Death In American Experience

Death
In American
Experience

Edited by Arien Mack

SCHOCKEN BOOKS • NEW YORK

Contents

THE "GIFT OF LIFE" AND
ITS RECIPROCATION

BY TALCOTT PARSONS, RENÉE C. FOX, AND VICTOR M. LIDZ

Introduction

A FEW years ago, two of us (Parsons and Lidz) ventured to write a rather general article under the title "Death in American Society." [1] For the present venture we have been joined by Renée Fox, and the three of us have decided both to extend the analysis of the earlier article and to narrow the focus. The "extension" consists in going considerably deeper into the background of current American orientations toward death and its meaning in the Judeo-Christian religious tradition than was attempted in the earlier paper. The "narrowing" consists in trying to focus on the institutionalization in America of the promotion of health and the care of illness, with special reference to the medical profession and its ethical orientations.

This focus seems particularly appropriate since the most important empirical argument of the earlier paper concerned the distinction between the inevitability of the death of every person, marking the completion of a full "life course," and the "adventitious" components of the death complex. The latter includes two types of premature death: that brought about by "impersonal" causes—for the most part disease, but also accident—and that imposed by what is in some sense willful human action, such as "violence." It is often difficult to draw a line between accidental and violent death, but the analytical distinction is crucial.

The most dramatic consequence of recent developments in health care has been—and within somewhat more than a century in

---

[1] Talcott Parsons and Victor M. Lidz, "Death in American Society," in *Essays in Self-Destruction*, Edwin Shneidman, ed., New York (Science House, 1967).

the "advanced" societies—the doubling, if not slightly more, of life expectancy at birth. To a degree never before true, it has become customary for the aware individual to expect that he will live to complete a "normal" span of life and for parents, that their children, if born alive and healthy, will also do so. The differentiation of the inevitable from the adventitious aspects of death has focused a more powerful light than before on the component of inevitability. If so much is controllable by human action, one must ask, what does it mean that there is nevertheless an absolute limit to our control? This problem of meaning, of course, bears with special cogency on members of the medical profession because they are *par excellence* the institutionalized trustees of society's interest in the preservation of life.

We will note that there has been in recent years a significant increase in both medical and popular concern with the "existential" aspects of death and also suffering. Indeed, the volume which Dr. Shneidman edited—part of a rapidly growing literature —attests to this fact, as does the greatly enhanced concern of medical students and physicians themselves.

The earlier Parsons-Lidz article used as a foil a paper by Peter Berger in which he claimed that the "denial" of death was a basic aspect of the American outlook.[2] We still think we were right in refusing that interpretation. We now believe, however, that it is not necessary to make an either/or choice between "acceptance" and "denial"; we believe that, as in many cases involving underlying conflicts, what is often interpreted as denial is in reality a kind of "apathy"—i.e., being in a situation of not knowing quite what to say or do and thus minimizing overt expression or action. This may also be reinforced by the "stoical" component of the Puritan tradition. We shall attempt to show how certain features of the medical situation and medical ethics have involved this kind of conflict with this kind of result.

[2] Peter Berger and Richard Lieban, "Kulturelle Wertstruktur und Bestattungspraktiken in den Vereinigten Staaten," *Kölner Zeitschrift für Soziologie und Sozialpsychologie*, No. 2, 1960.

On the positive side, we wish to re-emphasize what we consider the fully established view—that it is biologically normal for all individual organisms to die. Death is now understood to be an important mechanism enhancing the adaptive flexibility of the species through the sacrifice of individuals; i.e., it makes certain that the bearers of newly emergent genetic patterns will rapidly succeed the bearers of older ones. Death may be even more critically important in contributing to cultural growth and flexibility than in supporting genetic change. Thus, we may regard death as a major contributor to the evolutionary enhancement of life, and thereby it becomes a significant part of the aggregate "gift of life" that all particular lives should end in death. That is why it cannot be a rational pursuit of modern medicine to try to end or even minimize the "inevitable" aspect of death.

Our approach will emphasize theoretical continuity between the organic and the human socio-cultural levels, through the premise that the mortality of individuals has a positive functional significance for both human societies and the organic species. Beyond that, yet intimately related to it, is the fundamental distinction between, on the one hand, the "phenotypical" incorporation of genetic patterns in the lives of individual organisms and populations, and the genetic components themselves, and on the other hand, the modes and conditions of their preservation, implementation and development in the evolutionary sense. It is in this spirit that we devote our first substantive discussion to the field of *cultural* symbolization which in America bears on the problem of the meaning of death and, of course, its opposite, life. We think that the most important themes are found in the "constitutive symbolization" of the religious heritage.[3] To be sure, a substantial part of our contemporary population purports to "take no stock in religion." We feel, however, that the patterns of

[3] Talcott Parsons, "Belief, Unbelief, and Disbelief," in Caporale and Grumelli, eds., *The Culture of Unbelief*, Berkeley (University of California Press, 1971), Chapter 12. See also Robert N. Bellah, *Beyond Belief: Essays on Religion in a Post-Traditional World*, New York (Harper and Row, 1970), and his paper, "Religion and Social Science," in Caporale and Grumelli, eds., *op. cit.*, Chapter 14.

symbolization which we shall review have come to be constitutive of the *whole* culture by which we live, and that their relevance is by no means confined to the lives of self-consciously "religious" people. As social scientists we do not think that "science" in the usual sense has provided "functionally equivalent" symbolic patterns of orientation, though we think that the evidence just cited of the positive biological function of death and the recent enhancement of life expectancies is highly pertinent to our problem.

We shall be dealing with religious symbolism predominantly in the context of what has come to be called *myth,* in the sense used by Lévi-Strauss and Leach, and in another, related field, by Kenneth Burke and Northrop Frye.[4] We are not concerned with the problem of the historical veracity of the Books of Genesis and Exodus, or of the Four Gospels, but with clarifying the "structure," as Lévi-Strauss would put it, of certain of the themes expressed in such documents insofar as they bear on the problem of orientation to the death-life aspects of the human condition. Neither will we be concerned with the metaphysical question of the "existence of God." For us this belief is simply a basic element of the myth.

In addition, a principal theoretical emphasis has become much more salient than it was in the Parsons-Lidz paper, and has been especially emphasized by Fox in connection with her work with Judith Swazey on the "existential" problems involved in organ transplants, which will be discussed below.[5] This is the theme of the importance of the *gift* and of gift-exchange, as it was classically introduced into social science literature—though not without

[4] Claude Lévi-Strauss, *Structural Anthropology,* New York (Basic Books, 1963). Edmund Leach's little book, *Genesis as Myth and Other Essays,* London (Jonathan Cape, 1971), has been of important substantive as well as methodological significance to us, as has Kenneth Burke's *The Rhetoric of Religion,* Boston (Beacon Press, 1961). See also Northrop Frye, "The Critical Path: An Essay on the Social Context of Literary Criticism," *Daedalus,* Spring 1970, pp. 268–342.

[5] Renée C. Fox and Judith P. Swazey, *The Courage to Fail* (tentative title for a forthcoming book on organ transplant and hemodialysis, to be published by the University of Pennsylvania Press).

antecedents—a generation ago by Marcel Mauss.[6] It will be remembered that Mauss stressed not only the ubiquity, in human cultures, of the theme of the *giving* of gifts, but also how this *giving* creates, for the recipients of gifts, an *obligation to recipro-cate,* which on occasion can be onerous indeed.

In the following section of the paper it will be our principal thesis that in the Judeo-Christian tradition—and especially in the Christian phase—life, for the individual, is defined in the first instance as a *gift,* directly or indirectly, from God. It may be a niggardly gift, as with those born only to misery, want and suffering, or a munificent gift, as with those born with great talent and good fortune. Yet in both cases the gift of life creates an obligation to reciprocate. Our second main thesis will then be that the trend of religio-cultural development within this tradition has been toward defining the death of the individual, especially in the fullness of a complete life, as itself the gift which constitutes a full reciprocation of the original gift of life.

Not only may the obligation to reciprocate gifts be onerous, but the tragic view of the human condition has been in many vital respects structured about this onerousness. First, recipients must somehow be motivated to *try* to reciprocate: religiously, this commitment has, in our tradition, often been formulated as "faith." But the gifts, as we have noted, are by no means of equal value, and the sheer difficulties of reciprocation, except by "giving up," may be insurmountable. Particularly potent as a focus of tragedy is the fact that the fates of individuals are never neatly ordered in relation to those of the social collectivities in which they hold deeply meaningful membership. God is con-cerned not only with individuals but with "peoples" in the Old Testament sense. The problems of the beneficence or malevo-lence of God and of the shortcomings of individual human beings, religiously formulated as sin, are not to be neatly shoved aside by an equation of the reciprocity of gifts alone.

[6] Marcel Mauss, *The Gift,* trans. by Ian Cunnison, Glencoe, Ill. (The Free Press, 1954).

THE JUDEO-CHRISTIAN SYMBOLIZATION
OF LIFE AND DEATH

To the social scientist, the sequence "life-death" strongly suggests the "life-cycle" or "life-course" of the individual, sometimes formulated as "age"-grading or structure. But in alluding to this category, which includes both life and death, the social scientist almost automatically adds to the stimulus word "age," the words "and sex." With regard to individuals rather than species, these categories provide a frame of reference for analyzing the interface between the organic aspects of the human and the social, with the necessary relation to the cultural. "Age" connotes the passage through time of the individual, within the human-social matrix, from a beginning to an end. Since, however, individuals are mortal, the continuation of the socio-cultural system beyond the individual life-span depends on the mechanism of continuing replacement, through reproduction, of the passing generation. For man, as for almost all of the "higher" animal species, this mechanism is that of *bisexual* reproduction, with rather clearly differentiated biological roles for the two sexes in the reproductive process and, more problematically, differing roles at the social and cultural levels. "Age and sex" seem clearly to belong together in their biological and socio-cultural references. Sex is of course clearly dichotomously structured, while at first glance "age" may seem a linear continuum; but if one focusses on the terminal points of a clearly limited process, birth and death can also be treated as a dichotomous reference-base. Putting the two together we derive the familiar four-fold table of two dichotomous variables.

The myth of Genesis clearly embodies both variables, though in ways which are at one level somewhat contradictory. It is clear that God created man "as the Lord of the Creation" and "in His own image" to enjoy a very special status relative to the rest of the creation. In the first version, man is included with the animals in the formula "male and female created He them"; in the second, however, Adam was the sole human Creature, and when God saw that it "was not good for Adam to be alone," He created Eve out of Adam's rib so that they were of "one flesh and blood."

As Kenneth Burke [7] says, man, as the symbol-using animal, has the unique capacity of the "negative," i.e., he may not only assent, but also may say "no." There was one and only one prohibition imposed on Adam, and later Eve, in the Garden—namely that against "eating of the fruit of the tree of the knowledge of good and evil." Man, being even at that point what he was and is, defied that prohibition and, tempted by the serpent via Eve, "ate of the fruit." This was the mythical origin both of death—by divine decree at the point of expulsion from the Garden—and of sexual reproduction for humans, since in the Garden Eve was only companion to Adam, not sexual partner.

The symbolic implication of the Fall seems to have been a double one. On the one hand, the Fall was the simple result of disobedience to a divine command. On the other hand, having been told that if man disobeyed he would "surely die," it can be argued that Adam and Eve thought they could evade this consequence and presume to immortality, symbolized in the Garden by the "Tree of Life." It seems clear that "original sin" had this dual character—disobedience and the claim to an immortality which, since it was a divine prerogative, meant the claim to Godhead. The imposition of mortality on expulsion from the Garden indicates an emphatic divine insistence that man, as creature, was *not* divine.

At this stage the "gift" theme seems to be subordinate. To be sure, God gave life to Adam and Eve and enabled them to reproduce, through (in a sense) "compensating" them for their disobedience by giving them the "knowledge of good and evil." This knowledge has been interpreted by Leach [8] as comprising both knowledge of the inevitability of individual death, and knowledge of the "difference of the sexes," which can be further interpreted to mean the possibility of species survival beyond individual death

[7] *Op. cit.,* note 4.
[8] *Op. cit.,* note 4.

through bisexual reproduction. Both must, in our view, be interpreted as at once good *and* evil. The evil side, besides death itself, is embodied in the famous curses by God during the expulsion from the Garden—for Eve, condemnation to childbearing in pain, for Adam, the need to subsist "by the sweat of his brow." Indeed, a major biblical interpretation has held that the whole of human life since the expulsion could be summed up in the formula "sin and death."

Another theme, however, appears in early Genesis, that of a *mediator*. As Leach suggests, even the serpent may be interpreted in this light. Just possibly, God "wanted" Adam and Eve to sin, or at least was not too angry that the serpent seduced them. Further along, Eve, as the symbolically prototypical woman, becomes a kind of mediator, a theme which much later becomes central in the figure of Mary, Mother of God.

Meanwhile, the great theme of most of the Old Testament is not the spiritual fate of individuals, but the fate of a religiously-sacred social community, the People of Israel. Symbolically, they end as Yahweh's *chosen* people—but not without many vicissitudes. In the first major phase, God was basically displeased with His highest creature and contemplated destroying His entire creation, but relented to save Noah and his extended family. In a way, He purified mankind by the flood, leaving only the descendents of Noah to inherit—this was the first "Covenant." Following this came a series of further decisions, the most notable of which were the Covenants with Abraham asserting that his descendants should become the chosen people, and later with Moses, in a sense the main mythical founder of Israel. Leach has circumstantially analyzed the many vicissitudes of this selection process by which the People of Israel are said to have become established as a religiously-grounded socio-political community.[9]

Moses, however, not only led the Exodus from Egypt and renewed the Covenant of Abraham, but also introduced the Law as a major innovation. This came to be constitutive of Judaism

[9] Cf. "The Legitimacy of Solomon," in Leach, *op. cit.*

and, in a sense, of all its cultural derivatives. Throughout, little was heard of the "cure" of individual "souls," though such themes began to emerge in Hellenistic Judaism.

It should nevertheless be kept in mind that, not only by originally creating the human species but also by "choosing" Abraham and his "seed" and maintaining the Covenant with them, God gave his people the gift of corporate existence under divine sanction. This theme reappears later, in the conception of the Church of Christ and of a whole society as the "Kingdom of God on Earth." In the Old Testament, for the most part, both birth and death are treated within the framework of the sacred community, with the conception of death seen as "reception into the bosom of Abraham." The dead become honored ancestors of the living, with both incorporated in a time-extended, multi-generational community. As a background to the Christian phase, it is essential that the *permanence* of this community be assumed. There was no further divine threat to destroy it, as in the story of Noah; any further divine intervention would have to be different in character.

Early Christianity

It is a big jump to the symbolism of the much later Christian development, but our primary concern is not with cultural history but with a symbolic complex. There is a crucial difference between the relation of God to Adam on the one hand and to Jesus on the other. God *created* Adam in His own image, but Jesus was "His only *begotten* son." As just noted, we may infer that, by virtue of the series of covenants, God had committed Himself to the continuance of the human species, particularly but presumably not exclusively of His chosen people. His intervention in the human condition, therefore, had to be intervention in the affairs of humanity as "a going concern." Mary and the myth of the Annunciation is the symbolic focus of the divine recognition that "cooperation" with humanity is essential in order to carry out the grand plan. It is in this context that the very

critical symbol, blood, becomes central, referring to the continuity of human generations which, of course, assumes the death
of each individual together with the continuity of the population
through sexual reproduction, what the Old Testament calls
"begetting." The "blood" of Jesus had therefore both a divine
and a human component, the latter being the blood of Mary.

Within the framework of the People of Israel, continuity was
established in another way, through the role of Joseph as, in
Leach's term, Jesus' "sociological father." Whatever the theological subtleties of the problem of the Virgin Birth may be, Jesus
is forthrightly declared to be descended from Abraham through
Isaac, and most especially to be of the "House of David." This
genealogy is *through Joseph* (Matthew, Ch. 1), and the emphasis
on continuity in the sequence of generations is clearly another
reference to "blood" as an essential symbol of Christianity.

Another crucial symbolic note is sounded in the Christ story.
In Judaism, though Yahweh treated the people of Israel as His
chosen people, protecting them and favoring them in many
ways, His primary concern was with their obedience—that
is, their observance of the Law He had imposed upon them.
God was continually testing them, perhaps half expecting them
to "betray" Him. The severity of the testing may be said to have
culminated in the command to Abraham that he sacrifice his one
fully "legitimate" son, Isaac. In Christianity, the new note is
that of love, with its evident relations to the theme of giving. The
crucial Gospel statement should perhaps be quoted in full: "For
God so loved the world that he gave his only begotten son, that
whosoever believeth in him should not perish, but have everlasting
life. For God sent not his Son into the world to condemn the
world, but that the world might be saved" (John, 3: 16, 17).

It will be noted that God is said to have loved not only his
chosen people but "the world" as a whole. This universalistic
note could of course have a double cultural derivation, from the
Prophetic movement in Israel and from Hellenism. It is, in any
case, fundamental to Christianity. Salvation was still basically

contingent on faith—it was not to be open to "unbelievers,"
though the punitive tone of much of the Old Testament, as in
the phrase "The Lord thy God is a Jealous God," is very much
played down.   Perhaps, above all, salvation was conceived as a
gift *from* God, whereas earlier most of the giving had been the
other way around, as "sacrifices" *to* God and obedience to His
commandments.

In the New Testament there was a new conception of the
relation between the "eternal" and temporal orders, the divine
and the human.   Through Mary's "Motherhood of God," the
divine became human (John, Ch. 1).   Jesus was taken to be both
God and man at the same time.   This view fundamentally altered
the Judaic conception by making possible the upgrading of the
status of humanity—"the world might be saved." [10]   Again, in
spite of certain tendencies within Hellenistic Judaism, I think we
can correctly say that Judaism was not a religion of individual
salvation in the sense that Christianity is.   Burke has pointed out
that the idea of a redeemer is implicit in the Genesis myth, and
Leach has also emphasized the role of "mediators," but how the
role of the redeemer should be conceived and in particular what
the relation of this role to the fate of the People of Israel should
be was still very much an open question.

Here it is crucial to note that the founding event of Christianity
was mythologically the sacrificial *death* of Jesus by crucifixion.
Chrisitianity has traditionally held this to be a real death, and
not, as was common in Greek mythology, the mere disappearance
of a divine personage who had chosen to spend a certain amount
of time on earth disguised as a mortal.   Jesus really died on the
cross and had to be "resurrected" in order to re-enter the divine
sphere of eternal life.   It is of course central that the meaning
of Jesus' death was symbolized as *giving* His *blood*.   Blood is what
we may speak of as that *gift* of life which is above all centered
in the conception of maternity.   In the Christian myth Mary was

10 See also John 1:12, "But as many as received him, to them he gave the power
to become the sons of God."

the giver of life to Jesus, a specially symbolic case of the more general conception of a woman *giving* birth to her child. In ordinary usage the word "give" is not stressed in this expression, but we think it symbolically crucial. The human component of the blood of Christ, therefore, was a *gift* from Mary, who only in the more extravagant phases of Catholic symbolization has herself been considered divine. This human component, however, was combined with the divine component originating from the begetting of Jesus by His divine Father. In these circumstances Jesus' own death was relativized. The concept of death applied only to the human component, not to the divine. The symbol of blood is the primary focus of the unity of the divine and the human, the focus of the Christian conception of the transcending of death. Another meaning of the symbol, blood, which has Hebrew antecedents but was profoundly modified in the Christian phase, is reflected in the act of dying, which again was in an important sense voluntary on Jesus' part—that is, Jesus in a certain sense provoked the Roman authorities into crucifying Him. In the symbolism of the Last Supper, built into the basic sacramental ritual of Christianity, the Eucharist, there is not only the blood of Christ, symbolized by the wine, but also the "body" of Christ, symbolized by the bread. The body of Christ, meaning of course the risen Christ, came to be the symbol for the Church conceived as a supernatural entity embodying the Holy Spirit, which came to have the "power of the keys," the capacity to elevate the individual above the limitations of mortality and the other "Adamic" features of the human condition.

We do not think it too far-fetched to suggest that the Church was symbolically meant to "identify," in a sense not very different from the psychoanalytic-sociological sense, the ordinary human being with Christ. As a member of the Church, he became part of the "body of Christ" and thereby, *in dying* he became capable of *giving* his life, symbolized by blood, in a sense parallel to that in which Jesus gave His blood in the crucifixion. There seems to be a deep duality of meaning here: on the one hand, death is conceived to be deeply traumatic, symbolized by the suffering on the cross, and as such, a kind of "supreme sacrifice." On the other hand, the death of the individual can be conceived as not merely paving the way for his entrance into "heaven" but also as a sacrifice for the redemptive benefit of humanity in general. Quite apart from the metaphysical problems of what can possibly be meant by "survival" of the individual after death, this is a kind of positive sublimation of the grimly tragic view of the human condition as defined by the consequences of Adam's origi‐ nal sin. By the acceptance of the divine commandments and of Christ as the redeemer, man is not in principle totally expelled from the Garden to be dominated henceforth by "sin and death," but has the opportunity to participate in the divine order. He is thereby not in the Adamic sense *only* human. This represents a major upgrading of the religio-metaphysical status of man.

The collective reference has not been simply omitted here. It is through symbolic identification as part of the "body of Christ," i.e., the Church, that the individual can, even before death, par‐ ticipate in the "spiritual" as distinct from the "temporal" order. In a certain sense the old collectivity of the "people" became the model for a spiritual collectivity, membership in which was not by kinship but by faith, that is, acceptance of Christ. Yet Jesus was conceived not only as the "Son of God," but as "born of woman." His "body," though "mystical," was a means of mediat‐ ing between divine and human.

Furthermore, this pattern seems to underlie a theme in Western religious history which has been emphasized repeatedly in the literature: this theme is that the biblical conception that God made man in His own image and lord of the creation eventually materialized as the conception of a "Kingdom of God on Earth." This in turn implied that human society and personality could be permeated with a divine spirit, and thus the gap between the divine order of things and "the things of this world" was narrowed. What we have called the relativizing of the meaning of death seems to be a central part of this pattern. This is a relativizing that centers on the conception that every individual's death is both a *sacrifice,* and a *gift.*

The individual's capacity to die in the role of a giver of gifts [11] is dependent on three earlier and crucially important gifts. The first is the gift given by God the Father of what is sometimes religiously called the "living Christ" to humanity—given, it should be noted, through the process of "begetting" (Christ, after all, was God's only begotten son). It is of great importance that the giving of this gift was motivated by "love" of the world. Again, this was a gift to humanity *from* God, not a sacrifice *to* God. The second gift was the gift of life as a human being given to Jesus by Mary. The crucial symbolic focus of the Christian conception of the feminine role is that of "Mary, Mother of God," who has given the human component of the blood that is to be sacrificed for the redemption of humanity. The third basic gift is the sacrificial death of Jesus which has frequently been symbolized—for example, in the final chorus of Handel's *Messiah*—as the *giving of His blood* for our redemption. Within this framework, then, the death of the human individual can be conceived not only as a sacrifice *for* others, but also as a gift *to* others for the future of humanity.

The question now arises, what modifications of this predominantly Catholic vision should be introduced to take into account both Protestantism and more recent developments that are no longer predominantly Protestant? Before discussing the Protestant phase and what has followed it, let us sum up what seem to be the four principal steps in the development from the Book of Genesis to full-fledged medieval Catholicism.

1. It is clear that the original meaning of death was as punishment for the disobedience by Adam and Eve of the one prohibition imposed upon them in the Garden. Their sin, however, was not

---

[11] Cf. Talcott Parsons, "Christianity," in *International Encyclopedia of the Social Sciences,* David L. Sills, ed., New York (The Macmillan Co. and The Free Press, 1968). Most explicit is the case of the soldier or martyr who, it is said, "gave his life for his country" or for a "cause."

merely disobedience, but pretention to the status of divinity.
Mortality being the *primary* evidence of non-divinity, the imposition of death and expulsion from the Garden was linked with
the conception that this life should be burdened with travail.

2. With the development of the covenant relationship between
Yahweh and His chosen people, death took on a new meaning.
The biblical phrase is reception into "the bosom of Abraham,"
which we have interpreted to mean, in a sense parallel to the
Chinese tradition, that the dead achieve the honorific status of
ancestors in the transgenerational collectivity of "the people."
This is an acceptance of mortality as part of the acceptance of
the generalized human condition with all of its limitations but
with a note of special valence in the concept of chosenness. The
symbol of blood then emerges as a symbol of ethnic belongingness,
not only in one generation, but in the continuity of successive
generations. This in turn is linked with the special significance
of the Law as divinely ordained through Moses.

3. In the original Christian system, a major step in differentiation took place. There was a relative dissociation from an
ethnic community, with both the spiritual and temporal fates
of the individual acquiring a new salience. Human life, however,
is conceived as *given*. The primary symbol here is that of Jesus
portrayed as the only *begotten* son of God the Father. God's
begetting is quite different from the creation of Adam. It pre-
sumes the continuity of humanity and the human reproductive
process. Mary gives Jesus the gift of life at the human level,
and it is the synthesis of the devine and human elements, symbolized in the Annunciation, which qualifies Jesus to be the redeemer
of mankind. Blood in this sense was neither wholly divine nor
wholly human, but a special synthesis of the two which transcended the stark dichotomy of divine and human of the Book
of Genesis.

4. It seems clear, then, that the primary symbolic effect of
Jesus' sacrifice was the endowment of ordinary humans with the
capacity to translate their lives into gifts that simultaneously

express love for other human beings (as "neighbors") and a love for God reciprocating God's love for "the world." These are the two fundamental commandments of the Gospel.

There is, therefore, a profound sense in which the sacrifice of Jesus on the cross becomes generalized so that all human deaths can be conceived as sacrifices. The element of sacrifice, however, emphasizes the negative, the cost side, of dying, which was so salient in the crucifixion because of Jesus' excruciating suffering. The positive side is the *gift* not by Mary of the particular human life of Jesus but to any living human person of *his* life. This seems to us to be the primary symbolic meaning of the Christian conception of the transcending of death. Death acquires a trans-biological meaning because the paramount component of its meaning is the giving of life, at the end of a particular life, to God as an expression of love of God. This seems to symbolize the conception of a perpetuated solidarity between the bio-human level, symbolized by the blood of Mary, and the divine level, symbolized by the blood of Christ. In the ideal Christian death, one came to participate in the blood of Christ at a new level. This is the reciprocation of God's gift to mankind through Mary.

Protestantism

In the Catholic system this mutuality of giving as an expression of love was mediated by the sacramental system of the Church and from time to time fragmented by particularized absolutions. In the Protestant version, however, the sacramental system no longer had this power. The "power of the keys" was eliminated and the clergy became essentially spiritual leaders and teachers. Most important is that the life of perfection, the life which as a whole could be conceived to be both sacrifice and gift to God— namely, that of members of the religious orders—lost its special status, and every human being, layman and clergyman alike, was placed on the same level. We think, as Weber did, that this was basically an upgrading of the status of the laity rather than a downgrading of the status of the clergy. As Weber put it, "Every man was to become a monk." [12]

In one sense, the accent on life in this world was strengthened. This is seen in the Calvinist concept that it was man's mission to build the kingdom of God on earth. In this context the whole life of the individual was conceived as a unity. Its basic meaning was that of contribution to the building of the kingdom—that is, insofar as the individual lived up to religious expectations. His death then was *consummatory*, signalling the completion of the task for which he was placed in this world. This consummation, of course, required divine legitimation—i.e., through "faith"— but it also meant that in a curious sense dying became a voluntary act. A sharp distinction was made between dying in the ordinary sense and being killed. This conception is beautifully symbolized in a phrase in the Episcopal funeral service, "His work is done." (Also: "Well done, thou good and faithful servant.")

The implementation of the divine plan for the world brings the individual into a special kind of partnership with God. One might say that it completes the transformation from the Genesis conception of a life of travail following expulsion from the Garden and its bitter ending in death to the conception of life in this world as an opportunity to serve as an instrument of the divine will in the great task of building the kingdom. It is in this sense that Protestantism has been permeated with an acceptance of worldly life as basically good, and acceptance of death as the natural and divinely ordained consummation for the individual, but not the society.

There is, however, an underlying conflict. This positive and, in a sense, optimistic conception of life and death is conditional on fulfillment of the divine mandate—actually *doing* God's will. And this cannot be guaranteed. What Burke calls the element of the negative, the capacity to disobey, is just as characteristic of modern man as it was of Adam. The problem of what is to happen to the inveterate sinner cannot be avoided, because it

12 Cf. Talcott Parsons, "Christianity," *op. cit.*

cannot be guaranteed that sinners will cease to exist. Hence the note of death as punishment and its symbolic aftermath is always counterposed to this positive Protestant conception. Furthermore, no *given* state of society can be considered to be *the* "good society." Individuals must combat not only their own sinfulness, but the collective phenomena blocking fulfillment of the "Kingdom."

Another negative aspect is the consequence of the psychological connections between love and hate and the parallel conflicts at the social level. What psychologists call aggression toward others generally involves a desire to injure them or see them suffer injury, and in more extreme forms to see them die, even to kill them. Such wishes are also often directed against the self and figure prominently in the urge to suicide. All this is clearly contrary to the interpretation of the death of an individual as consummatory. Furthermore, conflict, accompanied by hostile wishes, between social classes, ethnic groups and nations is not easily compatible with the conception of a society as approximating a "Kingdom of God on Earth." Considerations such as these seem to have something to do with the extent to which populations with a culture close to the Protestant model are prone to rather violent fluctuations between moods of optimism and benevolence, and pessimism, hostility, and guilt.

It seems to us that the same basic pattern has survived the secularization which has led to the abandonment of the traditional Judeo-Christian conceptions of the role of the transcendental God in relation to humanity. The most conspicuous, though by no means only case, has been Marxian socialism, which—at least in its communist version—bears a great many resemblances to early Calvinism. Here the basic human assignment is to contribute to the building of socialism. The view of the fate of the individual "soul" after death is clearly different from that of a theistic Protestantism; indeed, in some respects it is similar to Judaism.[13]

[13] Perhaps the "bosom of Lenin" could be the equivalent of the "bosom of Abraham."

But the basic pattern seems very similar—that is, acceptance of mortality and the other fundamental features of the human condition, and, therefore, a conception of the completion of life, in the ideal case giving death a consummatory meaning.

Recent movements suggest a shift from the emphasis on "work" in the "Protestant Ethic" sense to a communally-organized regime of love which, of course, links with the earlier Christian traditions of love at both the divine and the human levels. It is not clear just how these movements are going to crystalize, if at all, but one thing is almost certain, that they will share with Puritan Protestantism and Marxian socialism a religious sanctification of life in this world.

One other important point should not be neglected. The early Christians were eschatologically oriented to the idea of a second coming of Christ and with it the day of judgment and the end of the world as it had been known to people of their time. The saved would then enter a state of eternal life in a new paradise resembling in some respects the Garden of Eden, yet different from it. The idea of some kind of pre-existent paradise in which man once lived has reverberated through the centuries, perhaps most conspicuously in the idea of the state of nature that was so prevalent during the Enlightenment. Rousseau seems to be its most prominent single exponent. A pre-existent state of nature, however, has been dynamically linked with the conception of a terminal state where all the problems of the tragic human condition are conceived to have been resolved. This kind of utopia has been exceedingly prominent in the socialist movement, most notably in the vision of communism as the end state of the task of building socialist societies.

There seems to be evidence that very similar orientations characterize the movement that one of us has elsewhere [14] called the new "religion of love." Indeed, in its more extreme versions the suggestion is made that a regime of total love can be set up in the immediate future. It will, however, have to be a terrestrial

---

[14] Talcott Parsons, "Belief, Unbelief, and Disbelief," *op. cit.*

regime which cannot conceive "the end of the world" as that phrase was meant by the early Christians. It could mean only the end of the evil parts of the world. We have the impression that a clear conception of the meaning of death has not yet emerged in these circles, but almost certainly there is a fantasy of immortality. Death, as it has been known since the abandonment of specifically Christian eschatological hopes, is somehow felt to be unreal and this conception may be attributed to the new versions of the centrality of previous human life.[15]

THE MORAL BASIS OF MODERN MEDICAL ETHICS

The Physician's Involvement with Problems of Life and Death

If modern man has experienced the religious dimension of his life in the world as a gift from God, he turns in secular contexts to medical practitioners in order to gain expert assistance in preserving and enhancing his personal giftedness. In contemporary circumstances, the physician routinely takes part in the "giving" of birth, makes the first survey of the newborn's "gifts," including announcement of sex, and begins to prescribe for the preservation of its life. In the early years, when life is deemed fragile, the doctor is consulted frequently by responsible parents. Throughout mature life, the individual has the positive responsibility as well as freedom to seek a physician's aid whenever his gifts are endangered by disease or severe stress. Perhaps this obligation becomes especially strong when aging begins to enfeeble at least certain capacities. Unless death arrives suddenly and unexpectedly, medical treatment will ordinarily be involved, and in any case a physician will "pronounce" the death. Within the course of the individual's life-cycle, the services of a physician are now often involved in many crucial transitions of life-stage and social status. Thus, medical examinations, discussion, and

15 Perhaps the slogan, "Never trust anyone over thirty," may be interpreted as symbolizing the "denial of death," since those living from age thirty on must become progressively more aware that the time will come when they will die.

prescriptive advice commonly accompany first entrance to school, the attainment of sexual maturity, enrollment in college, marriage, pregnancy and the birth of children, menopause, etc. Proper completion of such transitions in life status seems to require that a verification or determination of the giftedness of the individual be made by competent medical authority. Moreover, it is not unusual for relationships with a doctor to involve a diffuseness of concern for the welfare of the patient's life that is quite unusual outside the sphere of intimate primary ties—otherwise approximated only perhaps by religious-confessional and some educational relationships.

Modern, scientifically rationalized medicine may thus be regarded as a special set of instrumentalities and procedures for protecting the "gift of life." Not only does it penetrate very deeply into the routine social processes by which normal lives are constructed, but it is believed to act upon divinely given materials in circumstances of fragility, transformation, and danger. If the role of the physician involves not simply high status and honor but also a potential and frequently activated charisma of office, it derives these qualities from a fiduciary responsibility for maximizing those basic human gifts which individuals actually receive. In this respect the role of physician is closely related to that of teacher. In the context of the value patterns of instrumental activism that are institutionalized in modern society,[16] this specific type of responsibility constitutes a major normative structure in the articulations between religious premises and the secular social order.

The protection of the gifts of life involves practical efforts to control the causes of unnecessary and premature death. Despite this, the conditions under which particular deaths often occur represent the frustration of individuals' efforts to fulfill their personal roles in life. In a society that emphasizes occupa-

[16] Talcott Parsons, *The System of Modern Societies,* Englewood Cliffs, N. J. (Prentice-Hall, 1971). See also Talcott Parsons and Gerald M. Platt, *The American University,* Harvard University Press, forthcoming.

tional achievement as strongly as ours, this attitude toward death is perhaps especially poignantly felt when a promising individual dies in mid-career. The suffering and the disruption of the lives of others, generally family members, friends, and sometimes occupational associates, which usually accompany such a death must also be regarded as phenomena that hinder or reduce the realization of life potentials.[17] For many, the very prospect of death—especially in ways that symbolically touch upon powerful negative images in our culture, such as the degeneracy and loss of bodily control involved in cancer—produces horror that can substantially inhibit abilities to engage in many areas of social life. It is upon these reducible aspects or modalities of death that the life-enhancing efforts of modern medicine have tended to focus most sharply.[18]

Modern medicine can be distinguished from the practices with which most pre-modern societies have attempted to control the human impact of death by the strong specialization of its instrumentalities about the meliorable modalities of death. Modern medicine has tended to differentiate itself very sharply from religious, magical, and expressive means of orientation to the problems posed by death. It has tended not to deal directly with the existential issues of meaning raised by death. It does not claim to help patients deal with the "ultimate" problems associated with the eventual and sometimes imminent inevitability of their deaths. Rather, it has attempted to set such matters aside in order to develop specialized means of "treating" specific syndromes which are believed on scientific and empirical grounds to be "treatable."

Historically, this instrumental focus of modern medicine has been a difficult achievement. In many respects—for example, the continued competition of Christian Science, widespread fears in society of medical violations of the body, common suspicions about efforts to "treat" mental disturbances—it remains a partial achieve-

[17] Eric Lindemann, "Symptomatology and the Management of Acute Grief," in *American Journal of Psychiatry*, September, 1944, pp. 101–141.

[18] Here the concept of reducible death is an adaptation of the idea of adventitious death discussed in T. Parsons and V. Lidz, "Death in American Society," *op. cit.*

ment. Perhaps substantial tension resulting from forces within religious, moral, and expressive culture, which even now tend to place some limitations upon the scope of practice and treatment, remains intrinsic even to specialized, modern medicine.

Indeed, there appear to be some very strong factors operating within the cultural and social organization of medicine that are profoundly interdependent with the limiting cultural forces. Perhaps we have explicated enough of the interrelations between religious orientations and the patterning of medical practice to make it a conveniently paradigmatic case. It should be clear that religious orientations toward the meanings of life and death have comprised an important historical source of the instrumental activism embodied in modern medical institutions. Synchronically, the instrumental activism of the general religious culture contributes both crucial legitimation and patterning of commitments toward sustaining the pragmatically activistic institutional forms that modern medicine has developed. Here, the religiously-grounded commitments provide important foundations for the role performances of both medical personnel and the patients and their families who must cooperate with the special types of treatment that can be legitimated within modern medicine. Thus the special legitimation and value-commitments required by modern medicine seem to depend on the existence of congruent religious orientations in the broader society.

Religious patterns condition the practice of medicine in at least one other principal respect. Physicians, nurses, and other medical personnel, as well as patients who are severely ill, are confronted by the phenomena of death in massive ways. People in these roles must often carry grave responsibilities and make extremely difficult decisions, while acting under the stresses generated by impending or probable death. In this difficult situation, and perhaps especially for those who must routinely confront it, a strong religious or philosophical faith seems essential to sustaining legitimate commitments to role performance. The very specificity and instrumentality of the proper performances, which do not permit the primary emphasis on treatment to be compromised by direct involvement of religious concerns—to say nothing of "spontaneous" emotional reactions—add to the extent to which certain *underlying* commitments must be profoundly *serious,* in the sense of Durkheim's definition of religion as belonging to "the serious life." [19] They must be serious enough to maintain their integrity even when denied direct expression.

"Scientific" Medicine and the "Existential" Problem

A theoretical interpretation of the position of modern medicine must emphasize, then, both its comparative independence from direct or particularistic limitation by religion and its underlying dependence upon and penetration by religious culture.

What we now wish to examine is the comparable balance between independence and interdependence that characterizes the relations of medical orientations toward death with the general system of ethical beliefs in American culture. On the one hand, modern, scientific medical practice must operate independently of the diffuse processes of moral judgment in society. The physician's treatment of the patient is structured in terms of a professional exercise of applied science, not directly as a moral process of social control. The cooperative relation of physician and patient is often constricted, damaged, or undermined when the intrusion of diffusely moral judgment displaces instrumental calculation as the focus of treatment. Here, the modern physician's role contrasts sharply with that of the primitive witch-doctor or the archaic curer. There can be no presumption that the practitioner's efficacy is intrinsically bound up with the ways in which he exercises moral sanctions over the patient. Treatment is intrinsically technical and not dependent on moral judgment of the patient. On the other hand, the life-and-death responsibilities of the medical relationship impose strong moral exigencies upon all concerned just as inexorably as they raise religious problems.

[19] Émile Durkheim, *The Elementary Forms of the Religious Life,* London (George Allen and Unwin, 1915).

Hence, the treatment relationship must itself be controlled in terms of an autonomous ethical complex that is rationalized with respect to medical treatment that gives primacy to instrumental-technical calculation. Commitment to a specialized ethical system by physician, patient, and auxiliaries (e.g., the patient's family as well as nurses, aides, and hospital administrators) creates a crucial condition for stabilizing treatment relationships so as to offset the often severe and baffling stresses of uncertain diagnosis, treatment, and prognosis. Medical ethics have come to be rationalized so as to provide a set of categories of responsibility which can give general assurance that due care has been taken to protect the "gifts of life," whatever undesirable outcomes may ensue.

Although medical ethics require autonomy in adapting to the special moral problems of medical practice, they also require legitimation. And this can be gained only through integration with the general moral-evaluative system of the encompassing culture. In order to convey moral authority to specific medical practices and institutions, medical ethics must themselves be relatively congruent with the principles of the surrounding moral culture.[20] Moreover, the responsibilities and limits allocated to different actors—e.g., doctors and patients—must not conflict too overtly with the expectations structured in other specialized sectors of the moral system.

Our frame of reference is here specifically cultural. Broadly, we conceive a moral-ethical system as transforming religiously grounded premises or "themes" into more specific moral prescriptions that provide authoritative bases for the organization of institutions and the planning of sequences of action.[21] Obversely, the same processes of transformation must come to terms with the moral problems generated by the various institutional

---

[20] This conception of moral authority is developed out of Durkheim's usage in *Moral Education*, New York (The Free Press, 1956) and *The Elementary Forms of the Religious Life, op. cit.* See also V. Lidz, "Moral Authority," in J. Loubser, R. Baum, A. Effrat, and V. Lidz, eds., *Explorations in General Theory in the Social Sciences*, New York, The Free Press, forthcoming.

[21] *Ibid.*

operations affected by specific prescriptions. Moral-ethical functioning may be seen as simultaneously involving the "spelling
out" of the complex practical implications of general religio-
ethical principles and the reduction of these implications to certain consistent grounds of solution.[22] But problems of meaning
are continually raised by the impact of specific principles on a
variety of institutional situations and by the uncertainties which
specific institutional situations bring to bear on a variety of ethical
principles. Particular prescriptions generally draw upon a number of independent principles and have implications for a considerable range of interactive situations. Any equilibrium of
consistency concerning specific ethical issues is apt to be short-
lived, and problems of meaning are apt to reassert themselves with
changes in institutional conditions or even in other specialized
complexes of the moral system. Hence, despite the stability of
many major structures of moral-evaluative culture over considerable periods of history, ethical order at the practical level must be
a continually renewed achievement. Moreover, it must be
achieved specifically at the cultural level, that is, through the abstract and generalized rationalization of interrelations among
symbols, references, premises, principles, hypotheses, etc.

We interpret the religiously established theme of the great value
of the divine "gift of life" as comprising a principal premise for
medical ethics. Yet, it is important to recognize that it also com-
prises a premise for many other ethical complexes in our culture:
police activity protects the "gift of life," educational activity
serves to enhance the "gifts" of individuals, and automobile
traffic is regulated with a view to restricting the loss of
life—to cite only a few examples. However, as a general
construct within the moral culture as a whole—although not
necessarily in its bearing on medical ethics—the "gift of life"
theme has not generally established an absolute principle of

---

[22] Professor Lon L. Fuller has shown that the institution of adjudication performs
this function in settling legal conflicts. See his *Anatomy of the Law*, New York
(New American Library, 1969).

ethics. Thus, the general prescription of "give me liberty or give me death" has also been honored in American culture, and may even be said to have provided moral legitimation for conscription which has obligated men to risk their lives when the national freedom was believed to be in danger. Yet the moral authority of the "gift of life" theme is not simply overriden in this case. Ideals associated with the "freedom" of society have exerted powerful symbolic meaning and moral authority in part because of the willingness of many individuals to die for them.[23] Moreover, particular freedoms which can be viewed as more costly in lives than beneficial to society—for example, the freedom of private citizens to carry handguns—are apt to lose much of their moral authority. We may expect that leadership in efforts to redefine the scope of such freedoms will often be exercised by individuals whose special moral responsibilities to protect lives have been stimulated by social conditions. For example, physicians who repair many gunshot wounds in emergency rooms of large city hospitals are apt to be proponents of stricter gun control laws. The theme of the dignity of life not only enters a variety of areas of moral discourse but does so in a complex array of combinations with other evaluative premises, such as that of freedom. We must now ask whether similar conditions apply to the functioning of the "gift of life" theme within the realm of medical ethics.

We may suggest that the major burden of the articulation of medical ethics within the broader moral-evaluative culture is carried by the principle of the dignity and importance of *divinely*[24] given human life. Within the broad manifold of human activities, medicine takes on its special moral authority and somewhat charismatic status—qualities apparently essential for effective treatment in many difficult situations—from its com-

23 Cf. Henri Hubert and Marcel Mauss, *Sacrifice: Its Nature and Function,* Chicago (University of Chicago Press, 1964).

24 Here, as above, we use the traditional religious terminology. Let us, however, repeat our view that the relevance of these themes is not confined to religious "believers." Atheists or agnostics would simply phrase them differently.

mitment to, and ability to implement, this crucial value. Medicine is continually engaged in an effort to increase the level of rationalization of its instrumental techniques for protecting health and life against a very broad range of threatening conditions and sentiments. Similarly, there are constantly on-going efforts to rationalize medical ethics as means for assuring the implementation of the basic commitment to preservation of the "gifts" of life, especially through the allocation of firm responsibilities for the care of individuals. The functional viability of modern medicine, then, may be seen to rest upon a crucial constraint on the system of medical ethics, namely, that a position of strong predominance must be given to the principle of the dignity of life. Other principles must be firmly relegated to secondary positions of importance.

The maintenance of this structural arrangement appears to be quite problematic in two respects. First, the institutional ordering of treatment relationships requires that attention be paid to other principles of value in medical ethics. For example, there must be considerable emphasis laid on mutual respect between patient and physician, on honesty and fairness in communication, on limiting the costs of treatment to "reasonable" levels, etc. In many situations, and perhaps especially when illness is severe and/or treatment technically difficult, attention to these themes may conflict with the maintenance of a superordinate orientation to the value of sustaining life. Secondly, there is a latent or potential conflict between medical ethics and other sectors of the moral-evaluative system in which the principle of preserving life is not directly given the same priority. Medical institutions, therefore, require ethical means of assuring that actors involved in medical situations, including patients and their families as well as medical personnel, will in fact act upon the normative priorities given in medical ethics rather than upon some others. This exigency exerts strong pressure toward giving medical ethics an autonomous and clearly bounded form vis-à-vis other complexes in the moral-evaluative system.

If we may speak in somewhat ideal-typical terms of a classical form of modern medical ethics, its principal structural features appear to be understandable as adaptations to the functional exigencies we have just highlighted. The structural core has been an absolutizing of the value of preserving life. Both the life of the individual patient and the physician's obligation to protect or save the patient's life have been taken as *divinely given*. The physician could then take the obligation to attempt to stave off the patient's death as an absolute prescription—a "Commandment"—having no explicit limitations. Only the insufficiencies of the physician's instrumental resources would limit his effort to combat the patient's death. There thus has been very strong ethical motivation to increase the technical capacities of the physician in order to better implement his obligation to save lives under ever more difficult circumstances. Indeed, it would seem that the extraordinary growth in technical capacity achieved by modern medicine should be explained by reference not only to the general prominence of the value pattern of "instrumental activism" in modern culture, but also to the way in which instrumental improvement has served to ease severe tensions within the system of medical ethics.

Orientation to the nearly absolute "commandment" to combat the death of his patient provided a very strong and clear definition of the situation [25] for the physician in several respects. It assured the physician that he could act in direct relation to a value of great importance without having to embroil himself in a broad range of difficult problems of meaning. It permitted, indeed required, that he pursue the "saving" of life at almost any cost, that is, by subordinating almost all other value considerations. This nearly absolute commitment to preserve life strongly insulated medical ethics from any ethical system or complex that did not place a commensurate emphasis upon the value of preserving life, and thereby firmly grounded the autonomy of medical ethics. Finally, it offered a clear basis for disparaging any other ethical

[25] This is the technical usage of "definition of the situation" employed in Talcott Parsons, "Some Problems of General Theory in Sociology," in J. McKinney and E. Tiryakian, eds., *Theoretical Sociology*, New York (Appleton-Century-Crofts, 1970).

position, for it could reasonably be argued that no other position *really* respected the divine gift of life when hard choices had to be made.

Despite these impressive strengths, the classical ethics of modern medicine has contained some serious strains and weaknesses. One principal source of difficulty is that this ethical pattern allows little room for positive definitions of the significance and meaning of death. The primary meaning of death is structured to be seen as a medical defeat,[26] either for the physician personally or for the "state of the art" with which he is strongly identified. Especially when the circumstances are such that the physician is bound to "lose" many patients, he is placed under great personal strain. Empirical studies in hospitals have shown that there is a consequent tendency for physicians to be unable to give high levels of attention, emotional support, and careful treatment to their dying patients.[27] Often the attitude of the physician becomes extremely defensive just at the time when the dying patient and his family need assistance in managing the problems of adjustment to the impending death.[28] When the physician feels that he may have "caused" his patient to die by making a "mistake" in diagnosis or treatment, his burden of guilt (and perhaps fear of a legal suit or loss of professional standing) often severely restricts his capacity to treat and relate honestly to his patient.[29]

[26] Cf. Renée C. Fox and Judith P. Swazey, *The Courage to Fail, op. cit.*

[27] D. Sudnow, *Passing On*, Englewood Cliffs, N. J. (Prentice-Hall, 1967); Barney Glaser and Anselm Strauss, *Awareness of Dying*, Chicago (Aldine, 1965). Renée C. Fox, *Experiment Perilous*, New York (The Free Press, 1959) does not report the same conditions, or at least not in anything approaching the same degree. However, the patients in her study were gaining meaning for their deaths by being research subjects and, in dying, thereby contributing to the life of others in the future. This situation greatly affected their experiences of death as well as those of their physicians. Sudnow also reports conditions under which the stigmatization of dying patients by physicians and other hospital staff tended to bring about substantial relaxation of efforts to sustain the lives of dying patients. The strain also was manifest, e.g., in the "gallows humor" prevalent among the physicians.

[28] Elisabeth Kubler-Ross, *On Death and Dying*, New York (The Macmillan Company, 1969).

[29] Raymond Duff and August Hollingshead, *Sickness and Society*, New York (Random House, 1969).

Indeed, it seems that rather devious communication with the patient, often supported by other hospital personnel, is at least not infrequent under such circumstances. It also seems that many dying patients are better able than their physicians to orient themselves to the positive "consummatory" meanings of their impending deaths.[30] The physician may engage the patient in highly moralistic discourse, attempting to mobilize his "will to live" or his "fighting spirit" against death, even when death in the near future appears to be inevitable and the patient is more or less ready to accept his situation.[31] The physician may even make his continued close attention to the patient conditional upon a display of "fighting spirit" while the patient might prefer franker discussion of his prognosis. Treatment may be given more as a ritual commitment to the value of fighting death than out of rational expectation that it will help the patient. The patient's family—or indeed, the hospital—may be encouraged to make ill-afforded expenditures on such ritualistic treatment, while being discouraged from adapting their life circumstances—and especially their relationships with the patient—to the inevitable death.[32]

Exacerbation of Strain by Technical Advances

Some additional strains have been created by modern medicine's very high level of technical mastery, but these have become problematic for medical ethics only in relatively recent years. Despite the physician's "absolute" obligation to save lives and the givenness of the patient's life, the moral authority of the ethic is reinforced when the life being saved still holds much unrealized promise. Thus, medical treatment is generally undertaken with the greatest energy when at stake are the lives of children or adults "in the

---

[30] Kubler-Ross, *op. cit.*
[31] Duff and Hollingshead, *op. cit.*
[32] *Ibid.*

prime of life" or endowed with special talents or social responsibilities.[33] The physician's contribution to the patient's future fulfillment of promise or a calling comes to seem essential to the meaning of treatment. Under present conditions, however, it is not unusual that some of the most intensive and sophisticated treatment goes to aged patients dying from degenerative diseases. Often such patients can be kept alive only through massive artificial support, and have prognoses that do not permit realistic hopes of future fulfillment of a calling.[34] Sometimes treatment seems to contribute more to unwanted suffering than to preservation of the "gifts" of life. Under such conditions, severe problems of meaning are bound to arise within the classical framework of medical ethics, for the benefits of treatment are not obvious and the efforts to preserve life face comparatively rapid defeat.

The ethical focus on the obligation to defeat death through the mobilization of intense commitments and great quantities of medical resources has perhaps had some irrational effects on the development and allocation of medical resources. American medicine has become most clearly pre-eminent in providing the most intensive, most technically elaborate and "modern," and least cost-conscious treatments for patients who are already engaged in well-defined struggles with death or debilitating diseases. In this situation, there is a strong tendency to demonstrate—again in a fashion having a strong ritual and religious quality—that "everything possible" is being done to aid the patient. Notably, this is the situation in which doctors speak of themselves as engaging in "heroics." Such medical activity clearly makes a potent statement about the valuation of individual lives, both within medicine and in the society at large. Nevertheless, the stress on such medical heroics has diverted attention and resources from public health measures that, in other societies, have pre-

[33] Note the way in which President Nixon so strongly emphasized that Governor Wallace must be assured the very "finest" treatment and care after he had been shot.

[34] The religious phrase, "His work is done," might function as one possible standard!

served more lives at less cost—although leaving the physician with fewer "heroic" measures for the patient already struggling with death.

Emergence of New Definitions of the Situation

The strains we have just noted have been complemented by certain developments in medicine that tend to undermine the conception of the absolute givenness of human lives. One crucial area of change has concerned the understanding and definition of death as the "end" of life. Much attention has been given to the recent trend toward redefining death, so that brain function rather than breathing or heart function serves as the criterion of life. How this redefinition facilitates the transplantation of cadaver organs has gained much public notice. The broader background of this change is that a variety of recently perfected resuscitative and life-supporting techniques have confronted physicians with the routine experience of having large numbers of patients on the very border between life and death. Even early in their training, physicians now engage not merely in "saving" lives, but actually in bringing people back to life.[35] Large proportions of hospital patients lack, at least temporarily, the capacity to live but are "kept alive" artificially. Sometimes the decision to "allow" a patient to die by removing the artificial supports of life seems to be the most reasonable recourse, although it is a decision which physicians generally try to avoid. There are patients of whom it can reasonably be claimed that they have died more than once. Some transplant patients live only by virtue of the functioning of organs which were originally the "gifts" of

[35] The process of technical advance brings an element of relativity into the conception of the "inevitability" of early death. As a striking example, one of us (Talcott Parsons) remembers years ago hearing, on the occasion of attending ward rounds at the Massachusetts General Hospital, Dr. Arlie Bock, who was the "visiting physician," tell that when he was a resident, he administered the first insulin given in that hospital to a patient in a diabetic coma. It was the first time that a patient in a diabetic coma had ever recovered in the whole history of the hospital. In a certain sense this was almost literally bringing her "back from death."

another person.[36]   Although these circumstances have been the result of gradual, incremental improvements in medical technique, they clearly raise some new and difficult questions about the meaning and medical significance of life and death.

The problematic nature of the boundary between life and death has also come to involve the origins of life in conception and birth. Both contraception and abortion have, of course, very long histories. Yet, recent improvements in technique, if complemented by mass campaigns for "birth control," will make possible an entirely new level of mastery not simply of numbers but also of inherited traits of those born into society. Indeed, if abortion becomes widespread, already foreseen developments in genetic counselling will permit very considerable control over the inborn "gifts" of babies, and perhaps even their distribution in society.[37] The ethical issues posed by birth control, and especially by the abortion of viable fetuses, however, are very difficult to resolve. Most attention has been given to the question of when, in the development from conception to birth, the fetus obtains the "gift of life" which makes it an autonomous being entitled to legal and moral protection. Perhaps more interesting in our present perspective is the disjunction between, on the one hand, the pro-abortion arguments that fetal life may be terminated in the interest of furthering the parents' mastery of their own life circumstances or the environment in which they will rear children and, on the other hand, the absolute valuation of life within classical medical ethics.

Two other developments seem also to bear stressfully on the absolute conception of the givenness of life. One is the emergence

[36] Cf. Renée C. Fox, "A Sociological Perspective on Organ Transplantation and Hemodialysis," in *New Dimensions in Legal and Ethical Concepts for Human Research*, Annals, New York Academy of Sciences, 169 (January 2, 1970), pp. 406–428.

[37] It is an important feature of the process of differentiation under consideration here that an increasingly clear ethical distinction seems to be emerging between the moral status of contraception and that of abortion, at least beyond certain relatively early stages of pregnancy, although the boundary is not yet clearly defined. Even though the Catholic Church has so far refused to alter its historic position on either side, the change has gone very far indeed.

in recent years of surgical procedures, usually employed in conjunction with careful psychiatric analysis and treatment, for altering the sex of individuals.[38] Here, medical treatment is used to change the most diffuse and general of stable social identities that is ordinarily given with birth. The second concerns the treatment of individuals handicapped by markedly "subnormal" intelligence due to genetic causes. Together with increasing use of genetic counselling to minimize the number of births of such individuals, there has been a growing disinclination to place them in special institutions from birth or early childhood. Removing them from the general community may be interpreted as setting a certain boundary to the level of "giftedness" minimally characteristic of members of society. The tendency to reintegrate "subnormals" into the society, then, has the effect of somewhat blurring this boundary. Perhaps it is significant that persuasion of parents to keep their mentally handicapped children with the family has emphasized not only the benefits for the mental development of such children, but also the human pleasures and moral satisfaction to be gained by other members of the family.

That the increasing flux in definition of the boundaries of a human life has occurred at *both* ends of the "age" span seems to us to be particularly significant, as does the new possibility of deliberately changing biological sex identity. This seems to justify our focus, articulated at the beginning of this essay, on the "age and sex" frame of reference. Furthermore, the fact that there is a trend to include the mentally retarded in more normal social relationships is also very much related to the problem of the treatment of illegitimate children, especially by the institution of adoption.[39] Both of these developments relate to another of the main themes of our discussion of the religious background of the life-death complex, namely, that of the status of persons

---

[38] See Harold Garfinkel's sudy of a transsexual in his *Studies in Ethnomethodology*, Englewood Cliffs, N. J. (Prentice-Hall, 1967).

[39] Cf. Stephen B. Presser, "The Historical Background of the American Law of Adoption," *Journal of Family Law*, 1971.

and groups gained through "inclusion" in significant collective entities, both temporal and spiritual; one may also add the current intensive preoccupation with the status of the "poor" and of various kinds of "minorities."

The Restructuring of Medical Ethics

The pressures on the classical form of modern medical ethics have by now become so powerful that there is a quite widespread feeling that the profession must undertake a very general re-examination of its morals. In some quarters, there is exasperation—almost despair—over the difficulty of the problems that must now be confronted. Yet, we think the process of re-examination is already underway and that the outline of a new ethic is becoming visible.

The emerging medical ethic may be termed "a relativized ethic" or, in Weber's sense, an ethic of responsibility.[40] While this newer ethic has major continuity with the absolute ethic in making the principle of protecting life its highest value-premise, it no longer treats this priority as an absolute. Instead, the physician is given positive responsibility for calculating rational articulations between this principle and other evaluative principles recognized in the ethical system, so that normative prescriptions can be flexibly adapted to ethically difficult situations. The physician is no longer under an absolute commandment to preserve life, but may make a relatively free judgment—generally after consultation with colleagues, the patient, and the patient's family—about the extent to which treatment should be directed toward the preservation of life and the extent to which other ends should be given priority.

This form of ethics is more rational in that, by recognizing more explicitly the conditions under which direct struggle with death must be fruitless and even counter-productive in terms of other

40 Max Weber, *From Max Weber: Essays in Sociological Theory,* New York (Oxford, 1947). See also Talcott Parsons and Gerald M. Platt, *The American University, op. cit.,* Chapter 5.

values, it permits fuller implementation of a broad range of ethical principles. At the same time, it allows firmer action to be taken with respect to a broad range of the modalities in which death is socially disruptive. A further impetus to adopting the ethic of responsibility is that it provides a stronger basis for dealing with the problems of meaning which recent medical developments have been generating. However, this ethic imposes some very serious responsibilities upon the physician. He no longer has the emotional support of an absolute which gives him clear prescriptive guidelines. He can no longer externalize the ethical grounds of his action through comparatively simple logical operations. Rather, he must bear personal responsibility for the specific ethical grounds of actions. He must subject issues of the practical valuation of life, suffering, death, departure from social ties, the fulfillment of "promise," etc., to personal examination. In order to act honestly, he must often engage patients and their families in dialogues on these disturbing issues at times when they are apt to be profoundly troubled themselves.[41] These obligations do not make for an easy calling.

Change in ethical orientation to death seems roughly to index the extent to which the ethic of responsibility has come to prevail. The relativized ethic provides a greatly enhanced basis for recognizing the consummatory meanings of death. The impending, inevitable death of a patient need not be taken as a defeat of treatment. The efforts of the physician may then—in a certain sense—facilitate the patient's death, supporting his sense of dignity and his ability to put his affairs in order,[42] encouraging a readjustment in his relations with his family, and meliorating the trying conditions of a death. These activities also aid the patient to employ his "gifts of life," but involve the mastery of death as social and psychological rather than physiological processes.

The relativized ethic also renders the boundaries of medical

---

[41] Kubler-Ross, *op. cit.*

[42] We may recall the poignant words of Pope John XXIII when he clearly knew he was about to die, "My bags are packed, I am ready to go."

ethics more flexible in relation to other components of moral-evaluative culture. The physician must take more responsibility for admitting the medical significance of ethical considerations structured in other sectors of the moral system. The recognition of the consummatory significance of death is one example of the new penetration of medical ethics by a religio-moral perspective having essentially non-medical origins.

Perhaps the most massive recent penetration of extra-medical considerations into medical ethics has been the acknowledgement, partly under political compulsion, that the distribution of medical care in our society must be rationalized to a greater extent in terms of "health rights" which citizens hold simply by virtue of membership in society.[43] Here, medicine is adapting its ethical system to moral considerations of a predominantly political and legal character. However, it is clear that the long-run effect should be a substantial upgrading in the quality of medical care available to the citizenry at large, especially to those in the lower economic classes. In terms of medical ethics, this change must be adjudged a great victory. One concomitant of this victory—in certain respects a cost and in others a benefit—will be the further projection of medical responsibilities into the realm of public discourse. When massive social planning for new systems of health care is undertaken, medical advice takes on a new importance in public affairs. The fiduciary responsibilities of the medical profession then come to include the task of providing expert leadership for the public's deliberation on health policy.

It would be a mistake, however, to regard this extension of the medical role in any simple sense as only political. At issue are many questions of value with moral and even religious dimensions. Reformulations of quite fundamental aspects of our societal value system are underway which constitute its generalization and up-

---

[43] Cf. the conception of "social rights" developed in Talcott Parsons, "The Negro American," in his *Sociological Theory and Modern Society*, New York (The Free Press, 1967).

grading, not abandonment. The meanings of life and death are so centrally at issue that the medical contribution to the discussion seems bound to be substantial. If the ethical reorientation we have discussed becomes consolidated in the medical profession and is projected into the realm of public deliberations, perhaps medicine will provide the leadership in some very interesting developments in modern normative culture.

Most important for the theme of this paper is the fact that the direction of this change opens new areas of freedom for defining a meaningful consummatory death as the reciprocation of the gift of life which the person received at his birth. In addition to the enormous contribution of the medical complex in differentiating the inevitable from the adventitious components of death, and to the very great diminution in the incidence of the latter, this change may not only help to enable the dying person to leave in the spirit of a giver of gifts, but also may enable members of the medical profession to facilitate this definition of impending death instead of blocking it. The ideal outcome would be a coincidence of the meaning of the words we have already quoted—"His work is done"—for the roles of both dying patient and physician. The patient is hopefully "ready to go," whereas the physician has not only done his best to "save" his patient's life, but has complemented these efforts by facilitating a dignified and meaningful death.

THE "EXISTENTIAL" PROBLEM OF DEATH IN MEDICAL PERSPECTIVE

For social scientists who conceive "society" in a restricted way, the foregoing discussion of the relation of life and death to medical ethics might seem to "stand on its own feet" without reference to the considerations of the earlier part of the paper. We believe, however, that the trends of change in medical ethics outlined above are inherently intertwined with the problems of the meaning of life and death. Furthermore, we believe that the structure of mythic themes which we selected from the Judeo-Christian religious tradition constitutes the best available framework for understanding these phenomena.

Over the course of the past ten to fifteen years, what might be called the religious dimension of modern American medicine—its relationship to the gifts of life and death and their consummatory meaning—has begun to be more overtly expressed. Although this existential aspect of medicine is an irreducible part of its deeper significance in a modern society, as in all others, until recently the strong instrumental focus of twentieth-century American medicine exerted a repressive influence on its outward manifestation. Various social control mechanisms existed in the medical profession that actively discouraged involvement with so-called philosophical issues. In the medical school climate of the 1950's,[44] for example, faculty virtually never raised questions with students like "what is death?" "why death?" or "in what deeper senses, if any, does death differ from life?" Even in situations conducive to such querying—notably, the anatomy laboratory, the autopsy, or in the face of students' early confrontation with terminally ill patients—instructors rarely initiated such discussions. And if a student made a timorous effort to do so, he was likely to be silenced by classmates and faculty alike with the quip, "that's too philosophical." Decoded, this meant "the matters of which you speak are not sufficiently rational, objective, scientific, or pragmatic to fall within the proper domain of medicine, or of truly professional behavior." It was also characteristic of this decade that professionals were more inclined to speak euphemistically about the death of a patient—"he (she) expired," "passed on," or "was transferred to Ward X,"—than straightforwardly to state that death had occurred.

[44] These are direct, participant observations about American medical school milieux in the 1950's, made by one of us (Renée Fox), in her role as field worker for a study of the education and socialization of medical students conducted during that period by the Columbia University Bureau of Applied Social Research. *The Student Physician*, edited by Robert K. Merton et al., Cambridge, Mass. (Harvard University Press, 1957), was a product of that investigation.

In sharp contrast to such medical attitudes in the 1950's (at least in academic milieux where new physicians were being trained and scientific research emphasized), the late 1960's and early 1970's appear very "philosophical," indeed. Currently, along with an increased social concern about the inadequacies and inequities in our system of delivering care, American medicine is publicly pondering more existential matters: problems of uncertainty, meaning, life and death, solidarity, and of intervention in the human condition. In fact, one might almost say that a certain amount of "radical chic" now accrues to engaging these topics, most particularly that of "death and dying."

There are those who contend that this discernible shift in the orientation of modern medicine is due to recent biomedical advances—actual and anticipated developments in genetics and genetic engineering, life support systems, birth technology, including asexual reproduction, the implantation of human, animal and artificial organs, behavior and thought control—and to the problems of decision-making and longer range consequences ensuing from them. Although we would not deny the important role that these scientific and technological events have played in making the moral and metaphysical concerns of modern medicine both more visible and legitimate, we would maintain that the greater interest in such issues is part of a broader and deeper process of cultural change in our society. It is not only in medicine, for example, that concern about the "quality of life," equity, human solidarity and societal community is manifesting itself. From an evolutionary perspective, both the scope and intensity of these preoccupations in American society at the present time suggest that we may be entering a new stage of advanced modernity.

As fundamental as any changes in the meta-ethics of contemporary medicine is the process by which conceptions of life and death, in relation to the physician's role responsibilities, are being reformulated. Reverence for the gift of life, and dedication both to its protection and prolongation are still basic value commitments of modern medicine. If anything, in recent years physicians have been more vocal than ever about their disinclination to "play God," as they themselves put it: that is, to arrogate to themselves the right to determine "who shall live and who shall die," by making more vigorous and continuing efforts to prevent the deaths and perpetuate the lives of some categories of patients over others. References to the Nazi medical war crimes as the ultimate sacrilege to which medicine can be brought are often made in such discussions. What is implied is that, because the role of physician centers on knowledge that pertains to life and death, unless great moral vigilance is continually exercised, the equivalent of original sin will again and again be committed. And in the collective extreme, this can become holocaust. There are evident relations between these medical concerns and the persistence of adventitious death in war and by other forms of violence as these concern a more general public.

Nevertheless, the profession of medicine has been steadily moving towards a less absolute position on what constitutes sanctity of life and the value of preserving it. Serious attempts are being made to distinguish vital processes which maintain the individual sheerly as a low-grade biological organism, from those which are essential to "humanness" and "person-hood." The new operational definition of death now in the process of being institutionalized in the medical profession and the larger society crystallizes this distinction. For, in defining death as the irreversible cessation of higher brain activity, it codifies the position that although the heart may beat and respiration continue (either naturally or by artificial means), without neocortical function and the cerebration that it makes possible, essentially *human* life does not exist. Thus, in the face of irreversible coma, the medical profession now seeks and is progressively obtaining justification for declaring a person dead, and for suspending life-sustaining efforts on his behalf. It is the opinion of the ethical scholar, Joseph Fletcher, that this redefinition of death represents a cardinal step in what he considers an at once needed and desir-

able evolution of medicine from an ethic based on the unconditional "sanctity of life" to one premised on the "quality of life." [45]

These changes seem to us, in general theoretical terms, to be
interpretable as part of a more general process of "progressive social
change." [46] As noted above, they constitute processes of differentiation, e.g., from the "absoluteness" of the physician's obligation
to prolong life, to the opening up of several degrees of freedom
in this area, with the consequence of imposing new burdens of
decision on both physician and patient. There has been a process
of upgrading, not only of the technical levels of medical service,
but also of the opportunities to participate in a new "quality of
life" for sick people and others, as well as a process of "value-
generalization" by which the older formulae of the meaning of
life and death are coming to be redefined.

Perhaps as a harbinger of these changes, more than thirty years
ago one of us (Talcott Parsons) was startled, again at the Massachusetts General Hospital, by the sudden statement of an eminent
senior surgeon, "no, human life is not sacred." At first blush this
statement was wholly "meaningless." Fortunately, however, it
was possible—knowing the background of the remark—to interpret its meaning. The speaker referred to a case which he had
been discussing with his clinical clerkship group of medical students: it concerned an older woman for whom there was a "fighting chance" of gaining several years of good health and high
"quality of life" if radical and dangerous surgery were to be performed, while at the same time there was a serious risk that the
operation itself would be fatal. The alternative was a few more
years of living in a gravely incapacitated state where only a low

[45] This analysis and opinion were offered by Dr. Fletcher in the course of a
keynote address that he delivered at the National Conference on the Teaching of
Medical Ethics, held at the Tarrytown Conference Center, Tarrytown, New York,
on June 1–3, 1972. The conference was co-sponsored by the Institute of Society,
Ethics and the Life Sciences and the Columbia University College of Physicians
and Surgeons.

[46] Cf. Talcott Parsons, "Comparative Studies in Evolutionary Change," in Ivan
Vallier, ed., *Comparative Methods in Sociology*, Berkeley (University of Calif. Press,
1971).

"quality of life" would be possible. The surgeon's statement was his way of asserting the moral justification of deliberately risking his patient's life in favor of the chance of a really meaningful terminal sector—i.e., a chance of a period of "high quality" life as against a longer, more certain period of "low quality" life.

The Broadening of the Range of "Concern" for Medical Decisions

At the same time that the medical profession is outspokenly reluctant to make such God-like decisions, it is also increasingly confronted with the inescapable obligation to use its "new controls over life and death in a responsible way." [47]   One of the means by which medicine is dealing with this antinomy is through broadening its patterns of professional collaboration. In medical amphitheatres throughout the country, and in many conferences on medical ethical issues, physicians are discussing these aspects of their life-and-death responsibilities with psychiatrists, social workers, ethicists, theologians, lawyers, and social scientists, among others.   Often, these discussions turn around general principles and concepts, and *ex post facto* analyses of decisions about patients that have already taken place.   But, especially in university-affiliated medical institutions, it is also becoming more common for such consultations to be sought while the physicians entrusted with a particular case are still deliberating about the most rational and humane course of action to take.   Widening the orbit of colleagues whose advice they seek enlarges the range of expertise available to physicians, and provides them with intellectual and moral support from professional circles that are more than "strictly medical."

But perhaps the deepest significance of these more inclusive collegial patterns lies in their relationship to the closer integration with our main societal value system towards which the "new"

[47] Joseph Fletcher, "Our Shameful Waste of Human Tissue: An Ethical Problem for the Living and the Dead," in Donald R. Cutler, ed., *The Religious Situation 1969*, Boston, Mass. (Beacon Press, 1969), p. 248.

medicine seems to be struggling.[48] Partly independently of the basic shifts in these values, e.g., in the direction of their generalization, and partly as a consequence of them, medicine is now passing through a "time of troubles" and transition that centers on its growing capacity to sustain and abrogate life, its heightened tendency to raise questions of meaning, as well as of definition, about life and death, health and illness, and its greater concern with the equitable distribution of health care and scarce medical resources in our society. Through collaboration with other professionals, and also through the establishment of more collegial relations with patients and other consumers of health care, such as the families of patients, medicine seems to be reaching beyond the obtaining of counsel and consent on specific issues. A broader, more egalitarian moral consensus is being sought, that extends further than the "sacred trust" of traditional, one-to-one doctor-patient relationships, and the boundaries of what was previously defined as the medical professional community.[49]

Organ Transplants and the Gift Complex

In our view, one of the therapeutic innovations that most dramatically exemplifies some of the overtly or covertly religious as well as moral problems with which modern medicine is grappling, is human organ transplantation.[50] For, central to transplantation is "the theme of the gift," [51] a theme that we have shown

---

[48] This clearly requires careful definition and analysis. Perhaps the best reference we can give is to Parsons and Platt, op. cit., Chapter 2.

[49] We conceive this, theoretically, to be a case of the complex which includes differentiation, upgrading, and the inclusion of new elements in the previously more restricted complex. We suggest that, in the recent phase, medicine is less inclined to "go it alone" without the help of other groups in the society. With respect to the changing structure within medicine itself, in the direction of a more ramified complex rather than a single diadic doctor-patient relationship, cf. Parsons and Platt, op. cit., Chapter 5.

[50] This view of organ transplantation was first stated in R. C. Fox, "A Sociological Perspective on Organ Transplantation and Hemodialysis," op. cit. It is more fully developed in R. C. Fox and J. P. Swazey, op. cit.

[51] Marcel Mauss, The Gift, op. cit., p. 66.

to be fundamental to Judeo-Christian conceptions of life and death. With the possible exception of "giving birth," and to a lesser extent, donating blood, transplantation entails the most literal "gift of life" that a person can proffer or receive. The donor (a significant linguistic usage) contributes a vital part of his (her) body to a terminally ill, dying recipient, in order to save and maintain that other person's life. Because of the magnitude of this gift-exchange, and its symbolic, as well as biomedical implications, participating in a transplantation can be a trans-cendent experience for those involved, be it the live donor, the recipient, their relatives, the cadaver donor's family, or the mem-bers of the medical team. It may epitomize for them man's highest capacity to make the sacrificial gift of life-in-death, that is supreme love, commitment and communion. In this sense, re-gardless of how scientific the setting in which this transaction occurs may be, or how secularized the beliefs of those who take part in it, deep religious elements, some of them explicitly Chris-tian, are at least latently present in the transplant situation.[52]

Nevertheless, here, as elsewhere, the properties of gift-exchange are such that transplantation confronts medicine and the larger society with a number of phenomena that are more troubling than transfiguring. To begin with, live-organ (kidney) trans-plantation involves both the donor and the medical team in an unprecedented act, whose morality is subject to question: the infliction of deliberate injury on a well person, in order to help another who is suffering from a fatal disease. However noble their motivation in performing major surgery on a healthy donor,

[52] So far, especially in the more radical transplant situations, the relations of living donor and recipient have been mainly "particularized," i.e., occurring between close relatives. In the case of cadaver donors, the identity of whom is concealed from the recipients and their families, the possibility has begun to emerge of something like "organ banks" in which organ "deposits" would be made, and withdrawals from them would be wholly impersonal—merely "equating" the functional capacity of organs with recipients' needs. How far such a development can go and what its consequences might be are problems on the fringe of the present discussion.

the medical profession thereby compromises one of its basic, shall we say "absolute," ethical tenets: "to do no harm." [53]

Furthermore, under the circumstances in which live transplantations normally occur, the quality of consent obtained from the donor and recipient for this still experimental procedure is often strained. A family member is dying of renal disease, and his best chance for survival with a tolerable life is to be the recipient of a kidney from a relative whose tissue-type closely matches his own. No matter how scrupulously low-keyed and sensitive the medical team's process of screening candidates may be, the fact remains that, in this predicament, prospective donors are under very great inner and outer pressure to give an organ to their suffering relative who, in turn, is under extraordinary pressure to receive one. Thus, the norm of "voluntary informed consent" can only be imperfectly realized.

And what constitutes so-called healthy, positive motivation, either in life or in death, for someone to donate a part of his body to a known or unknown other? Here, the medical profession has been brought face to face with the question of how much faith they collectively have in the altruistic principle, and how much belief in the desire and capacity of human beings to relate to one another as their "brothers' keepers" and as their "strangers' keepers," [54] which in Christian parlance may be phrased as "loving their neighbors."

Still another set of value-questions that transplantation has raised turns around the allocation of scarce resources. Who should be the beneficiaries of the limited supply of human organs for transplantation that are made available through donation? What criteria of choice, if any, would be compatible with the highest value-commitments of our society? More fundamentally still, ought we to be expending so many material and immaterial resources for this kind of confrontation with terminal illness and

[53] This is perhaps to say that the striking increases in the potential to promote life at the same time imply risks and costs which may endanger life.

[54] Richard M. Titmuss, *The Gift Relationship: From Human Blood to Social Policy*, New York (Pantheon Books, 1971), *in passim*.

death, when we might be investing them in the more universalistically life-giving purpose of providing good health care for our entire citizenry?

But perhaps the most chastening discovery that medicine has made about the gift relationship established by transplantation is that it can bind donor, recipient and kin to one another, emotionally and morally, in ways that are likely to be as fettering as they are liberating. Giving and receiving life in this form can lock the participants into an encompassing creditor-debtor relationship that blurs their separate identities, and diminishes their ability to reach out to others. Herein lies the potential tyranny of the human gift, its paradox, and perhaps its ultimate religious mystery. Organ transplantation suggests that the only perfect, truly redemptive gifts are *divine* ones. These are gifts of life and death from God, which constitute the at once sacred and flawed materials on which medicine acts: our essential humanity. The threat is to compromise the universalistic thrust of modern values.

Conclusion

We hope we have been able to draw certain lines of connection between some very ancient themes defining the human condition with reference to life and death, and some very immediate developments, with special reference to the orientations, functions and obligations of the contemporary medical profession.

Our primary theses are, first, that the problem of the meaning of death has been coming more and more explicitly to the fore in the recent development of our culture, and that a major focus of this salience has been in the medical world. Secondly we feel that, new as these developments are, they are not understandable except in reference to the great religious tradition of our culture, especially as expressed in the major constitutive "myths."

The theme of gift-exchange between God and man has been central to our analysis. In particular, we have emphasized the salience of the conception that human life is a gift from God. We have then, we think, been able to trace at least in outline the evolution of the conception that the death of the individual, at the close of a "full" life, not only *may* be, but in fact often *is*, interpreted as a reciprocal gift to God, the consummatory reciprocation of the gift of life. The emergence of this interpretation, we believe, has been enormously facilitated by medical control over the causes of adventitious death.

All of this has been occurring in the context of the development of a highly rationalized, technical, industrial society. "Scientific medicine" has been part and parcel of this society. The involvement, however, of the medical profession in the existential problems of the meaning of life and death, and at least its tentative movement in the direction of incorporating such a dimension, seems to us to be a striking example of the intimate interweaving of the more rationalistic and the more existential components in the development of modern society and culture. Far from there being a necessity to choose between the "scientific" attitude toward illness and health, life and death, and a "mystical" orientation, we hope that we have made a modest contribution to understanding the ways in which a synthesis of these two aspects of modern culture may be possible.

THE PREMATURE GERONTOCRACY:
THEMES OF AGING AND DEATH
IN THE YOUTH CULTURE

BY DAVID GUTMANN

I. INTRODUCTION: THE YOUTHFUL FIXATION ON DEATH

THE young people of the counter-culture now obsessively use the terms "life" and "death" to make political, moral, racial, and even generational distinctions. Thus, "life-loving," "life-enhancing," or "of the camp of life" are used to refer to those who are young, black, left-wing, or proletarian; while "the camp of death" includes the bourgeois, the white-skinned, the politically liberal or conservative, and the middle aged (though not the old). This rhetoric has its uses: it takes away the horror of death by presenting it as an invention of the establishment, a side effect of Con I and Con II. In addition, this language reduces the moral ambiguity of revolutionary politics—it is comforting to believe that the killing that is a necessary part of revolution is done in the name of nothing less than *life* itself.

But the "life—death" rhetoric does more than justify violence or defend narcissism: it is expressive as well as defensive. It seems to express fears, preoccupations, perhaps even fascinations with death, on the part of a young, liberated and usually gifted cohort. And when we look at the rising number of casualties among the new youth from drug over-dose, serum hepatitis, and VD, then we have to consider the possibility that some of our most promising children are driven to risk death, and even to suffer it. Behind the "kids'" strident accusation that the establishment forces them towards various forms of death, there may well be some unacknowledged lethal impulse of their own.

This tragic paradox—that those who stand at the beginning of life should share the concerns of those whose lives are ending—is usually explained by the probability of destruction in an atomic war. No doubt this fear plays a large part: young people, with all their lives before them, have the most to lose in a holocaust, and so are most oppressed by the sense of doom. However, it appears to me that there are other, less rational and less apparent reasons for the youthful preoccupation with death. These have to do with the psychological resemblances between the very old and the youthful counter-culturists that have impressed me in the course of carrying out research on the comparative psychology of aging.

II. THE NORMAL PSYCHOLOGY OF AGING: A BACKGROUND SUMMARY

This argument—that there is a psychological equivalence between the new youth and the old men—calls for a short review of the psychological events in normal aging. Accordingly, I will lead off with some observations and findings concerning the psychological traits which seem to be most characteristic of older men, those aged 60 and over, regardless of culture. The cited research into what might be called the species psychology of aging has occupied me for the past eight years, and has involved intensive interviewing and projective testing of men from various ethnic and cultural groups: urban, middle-class white Americans; Mayan Indians of Yucatan and Chiapas; traditional (Western) Navajo Indians; and Druze agriculturalists of the Galilee and Golan Heights.[1]

Except for the urban American group, the subjects are drawn

1 The over-all program of cross-cultural research has been supported by Career Development Award No. 5-K3-Hd-6043 from the National Institutes of Child Health and Human Development. Field expenses for Indian studies in Mexico and America were covered by Faculty Research Grants Nos. 1344 and 1412 from the Rackham School of Graduate Studies, The University of Michigan; and by grant No. MH 13031-01 from the National Institutes of Mental Health. Field work expenses among the Druze were covered by grant No. M66-345 from the Foundation's Fund for Research in Psychiatry.

from traditional societies which, while they differ from each other as regards the content of culture, have in common a conservative orientation towards social change. It is either resisted, or it proceeds at a relatively slow pace.

The guiding hypothesis of this study is that age-group comparisons between younger men (aged 35–54) and older men (aged 55–85±) carried out within traditional societies will reveal patterns of psychological difference between these age cohorts similar to those originally found in a population of middle-aged and middle-class white, urban Americans. The predicted finding, of universal patterns of age differences, clearly cannot be explained in extrinsic or socio-cultural terms, since the societies studied tend to be stable; and such cultural change as does take place has a different direction at each site. Furthermore, if the same variables tend to discriminate age groups across cultures, such variation cannot be ascribed to the influence of particular cultural age-grading systems, since the normative content of these systems also varies across the sites. Positive findings force us to think in terms of the human life-cycle as an independent event that has some fixed psychological implications; they make us think in terms of internal, mandatory programs of change that will shape thought, imagery, and behavior in predictable ways, across a wide variety of cultures. Accordingly, such comparisons, between age cohorts and across cultures, tell us something about a piece of refractory human nature—the species psychology of aging. Aging is also the prelude to death, and to the degree that death is also a personal, psychological event, the study of the normal psychology of later life may also tell us something about the normal psychology of dying. Finally, if there are some fundamental parallels between the themes of aging and those emerging in the youth culture, this comparative analysis may provide some insight into the meaning of that much debated sub-culture; and by extension, into the death-consciousness prevalent in its youthful members.

The phasing out of Aggression

The methods and the results of the various cross-cultural studies summarized here have been reported in detail elsewhere.[2] This paper will report only a summary of the major results. Turning to these, the firmest findings point to the almost universal phasing out of aggressive motives in men during late middle life, and their replacement by more tender, affiliative sentiments. Thus, we find that older men abjure competition, avoid provocation, and only enter into conflict situations as peace-makers. The major advice given to their sons by older men is that they should avoid quarrels and fights. Thus, in societies where liquor is used, young men are urged to avoid the strong drink that leads to combat and its possibly lethal consequences. However, while older men may become less aggressive in their behavior and attitudes towards others, their concern with aggression *per se* does not end. It is still something to be reckoned with, but now as an external rather than as an internal threat. This is in contrast to younger men who are more preoccupied with the management of their own rather than others' aggression. For my younger subjects, aggression is *internal,* and potentially at their disposal. It is energy, and, as such, capable of good or bad, constructive or destructive uses. As the younger men see it, their job is to maintain internal controls in order to ensure that their energy will be put to good rather than bad uses. For older men, energy still mingles both beneficial and destructive potential, but now

[2] See D. Gutmann, "An Exploration of Ego Configurations in Middle and Later Life," in B. Neugarten, ed., *Personality in Middle and Later Life,* New York (Atherton, 1964); "Mayan Aging—A Comparative TAT Study," *Psychiatry,* 29 (1966), pp. 246–259; "Aging among the Highland Maya: A Comparative Study," *Journal of Personality and Social Psychology,* 7 (1967), pp. 28–35; "The Country of Old Men: Cross-Cultural Studies in the Psychology of Later Life," in W. Donahue, ed., *Occasional Papers in Gerontology,* Ann Arbor (Institute of Gerontology, University of Michigan, 1969), pp. 1–37; "The Hunger of Old Men," *Trans-Action,* Vol. 9, Nos. 1–2 (November–December, 1971), pp. 55–66; D. Gutmann and A. Krohn, "Changes in Mastery Style with Age: A Study of Navajo Dreams," *Psychiatry,* Vol. 34, No. 3 (August, 1971), pp. 289–300.

it is at the disposal of external agents—their grown sons, the priests, the gods, witches, village authorities, even their wives— who can help them or harm them at their pleasure. The older man's job is to manage power in its external manifestations, to ensure that the good powers will intercede in their behalf against the bad powers that menace and frighten them. Accordingly, the aging man often moves away from a provocative, confronting stance and towards one that is, outwardly at least, accommodating, propitiatory and even humble, particularly towards the holders of power. Their implicit message to power-bearers is: "I am no threat, and I deserve your helpful intervention."

The Turn From Productivity To Receptivity

Younger men have to contain their boisterous aggression, and channel it towards productive applications: they either create or take charge of the resources vital to their own security and the security of their dependents. Apparently, the experience of marriage and fatherhood gives them the incentive to make the difficult switch from a combative to a more disciplined and productive deployment of their vital energies. They become builders, instead of fighters and potential destroyers. But with older men, the current sets in the opposite direction, towards passivity. Older men are counter-aggressive; and they also tend to be counter-productive. Instead of being a source of security to others, they come to rely on various forms of security, emotional and material, that are provided for them by others. Thus, they become dependent on the productive activity of their grown sons, their wives, the priests, supernatural helpers, social agencies —the particular nature of the nutritive agent has to do with their cultural customs, and with their personal circumstances. The important thing is that older men turn—whether with pleasure, with shame, or with apprehension—towards a receptive and away from a productive position.

The Sensuality of Later Life

This emerging receptivity is not restricted to human relations alone. Older men are not only receptive to love and support from human providers; they also draw supplies from the impersonal world. For example, *concerns* about food become increasingly important to aging men: they think about food, they reminisce about it, and while their actual intake may decline, they become increasingly picky about their grub. Older men tend to become food faddists, and they become particularly addicted to those foods that they first received from their mothers, in early childhood.

Younger men mainly love what they have produced, but older men respond to all the small pleasures that nature provides: pleasant sights and sounds, soothing textures, warmth and sunshine. Thus, younger men looking at their corn field will see a cash crop; they see money growing. Older men will look at their corn field in less utilitarian, less instrumentalized ways. They report the beauty of the fresh green leaves, the softness of the corn silk, and the plumpness of the kernels. Young men see a product, a piece of security that they have generated; but old men take pleasure in the corn itself, through all their senses.

III. A DEVELOPMENTAL THEORY OF ADULTHOOD AND OLD AGE

One general and obvious conclusion that can be drawn from the observed age differences is that young men repress their sensuality, they delay gratification, and that older men are less likely to impose these restraints on themselves. In these relatively affluent times we are likely to appreciate the sensual "switched on" old man over the utilitarian, "tuned out" young man. But psychoanalytic theories of development hold that the forms of repression maintained by younger men are vital to survival, particularly in the face of the average expectable human condition of scarcity and necessity. Briefly stated, Freudian theory holds that young men transform their bodies into tools and weapons by developing the capacity for delay of gratification, that is, by clearing their muscles, skin, and sphincters of sensitivity to pleasure. Sensuality is fenced off, relegated to the genital zone, there to be experienced intensely but briefly and in the service of procreation. If this process of repression, of internal boundary-building succeeds, then young men are able to face the challenging and often dangerous world of enemy, prey or hard work without being distracted by too much longing for comfort or security. By and large, they can be trusted to do what has to be done, or what their elders and leaders tell them has to be done. This repressive process is strongly stimulated and reinforced in men by the experience of parenthood. Apparently, the vulnerability and helplessness of infants and young children arouses a sense of chronic emergency in parents (even under relatively affluent conditions), one that fathers and mothers respond to in sex-specific ways. Thus the young father reacts to that emergency by forcing even further into his psychic underground the receptive sensuality that could be distracting for him in his instrumental role, and hence potentially lethal to his children. These dangerous promptings are also handled by giving them over to an indulged and dependent wife, and by living them out vicariously through her. The wife becomes an external representation of the "passive" yearnings that the father must give up in order to provide security to others; and by the same token the wife concedes to her husband— and figuratively sends out of the house with him—the aggression that could be lethal, in the emotional and even in the physical sense, to her vulnerable offspring.

In sum, the needs of vulnerable children seem to be a formidable stimulus to fathers as well as to mothers—paternity as well as maternity has its imperatives—and the standard reaction *for each sex* is to surrender to the other the qualities that would interfere with the provision of their special form of security. Men, the providers of physical security, give up the sensual dependency that would interfere with their courage and endurance;

and women, the providers of emotional security, give up the aggression that could frighten or hurt a vulnerable, needful child.[3]

An Outcome of Normal Development: The Unisex of Later Life

In any event, the period of chronic emergency passes; children grow up, develop their own capacity for active mastery, take over the responsibility for providing their own security and, in some particularly orderly and traditional societies, the security of their parents. The general consequence is that both sexes can afford, in later life, the luxury of living out the potentials and pleasures that they had to relinquish early on, in the service of their particular parental task. A massive involution of middle life takes place, wherein, as we have described, men begin to live out directly, to own as part of themselves, the passivity, the sensuality, the tenderness—in effect, the "femininity"—that was previously repressed in the service of productive instrumentality. By the same token, we find (across a vast range of societies) the opposite effect for women, who generally become domineering, independent, and unsentimental. Just as men reclaim title to their denied "femininity," women in late middle life repossess the "masculinity" that they once had to send out of the house, and live out vicariously through their husbands.[4]

---

[3] Clearly, the usual sex-role distinctions which define women as more "passive" than men were not invented to swell the egos of chauvinist males; they are an adaptation suited to provide young children with a secure, "average expectable" psychosocial environment. It may well be that increasing numbers of battered children in our society is the price that we pay for early unisex. When young mothers keep title to their aggression instead of sending it out of the house with their husbands, they may become directly lethal to their infants.

[4] Women's lib only forces the natural pace towards unisex. The revolution in sex-roles that the sisters desire is eventually provided to most women by the fixed sequences of the life-cycle. Men and women are not separated by unchanging patterns of "masculine" and "feminine" traits; rather, they are distinguished by the temporal staging of these traits: men can be defined as the sex who are masculine *before* they exhibit the cluster of relationship capacities and sentiments that we know as "femininity," and women can be defined as the sex for whom this sequence is reversed.

The consequence of this mid-life involution is that the sexes move closer together, psychologically, each partner becoming what the other used to be, and there is ushered in the unisex of later life. Thus, the loss in later life of boundaries and distinctions within the self is matched by the blurring over of inter-sex distinctions, and by the fading out of the tensions that once charged sexual relationships with their sense of drama and excitement.

The Religiosity of Later Life

Since women are reputed to be more devout than men, the "feminization" of older men may partly account for their evident swing towards religion. But whatever the causes, the religious bent of older men is clear. It shows up in many ways, depending on the religious structure of the society. For example, Druze men of about age 60 are likely to be inducted into the ranks of the religious elite—the *Aqil*—those respectful men who know the esoteric secrets of the Druze religion. But even in societies without a pervasive religious life, we can see the development, in dreams, or in responses to our projective tests, of a *sub rosa* religious orientation among older men. Thus, when younger men look at a TAT picture of a man with his arm extended, they say that he is threatening or hitting somebody. But older men, even in cultures which do not sponsor a formal religious role for their age-grade, see this same figure extending this same arm beseechingly, and in prayer. Along similar lines, old men are more apt than younger men to believe that *particular* deaths or misfortunes are caused by witches or other supernatural agencies, even in societies where the belief in such agents is general across age groups. In the relatively primitive Mayan and Navajo cultures, old men see life as a drama between the evil spirits and the good influences that can be called up, through prayer and humility, to serve as buffers against the malignant powers. The more sophisticated Druze do not fraction external power into good and bad agents, but see all events, whether lethal or benign, as coming from the same Allah, whose purposes are unknowable but also perfect.   In both cases, Indian and Druze, older men are taking a humble, deferential stance towards great power, which is seen to be outside of themselves, and to which they need to be allied.   Where young men seem to feel that they must—by effort and risk—generate internal power, older men seem to feel that they can *cajole* external power to their aid through postures of submission, and demonstrations of weakness.   In prayer they pantomime the postures that the gods would require of them.

Religion as Vicarious Production

But the religious bent of older men has other sources besides the wish to gain security through submission.   It has sources in the ego as well as in the id.   Thus, men of all ages need to feel that they participate in some central, excellent and productive order of the universe.   This need to be in touch, whether in active or passive ways, with good and productive forces does not end as the individual life-cycle turns towards its final station. As men sense the ending of their own individual cycle, they tend to identify themselves with other productive cycles that began before them and that will continue after them; cycles that do not end with death, but that persist through *and because of* alternations of death and rebirth.   Thus, older men tend to move away from defining and implementing their own productive purposes, and they put themselves at the service, at least in token ways, of the productive forces of the universe, as these are represented in their culture. Where young men live out their passivity vicariously, through their wives, old men live out their active productivity vicariously, through their association with the gods. Specifically, I find that old men are interested in growing things, not solely for purposes of profit but in order to feel that they are agents of some larger productive principle that is manifested through themselves.   Thus, older Navajos, as mentioned earlier, will see beauty in an ear of corn, not because it represents money or sustenance, but because it grew from a seed. Aging executives in Kansas City will turn, moved by the same sentiments, to the cultivation of rose bushes.

Older men also become more tender and "maternal" in their relations with young children (the "grandfather syndrome"). This probably has to do with the previously discussed "femininity" of later life; but older men—who are trying to escape from the sense of the *end*—also appreciate children because they stand at the *beginning*. Thus, in their involvement with children, old men seem to revive the climate of their own beginning. But at the same time, through their concern for children, old men revive the sense of what Erikson [5] has called *generativity*—the sense that they are agents in some larger process of natural growth.

I would submit that as older men try to identify with versions of productivity that are outside of themselves, they become, in the best sense of that word, religious; and in their attempt to personalize, to give shape and substance to a principle that they only dimly apprehend, they are led naturally towards the religious imagery of their culture, and so into conventional religious affiliation. The paradox lies in the fact that this affirmation of life through care-taking and religious practices is predicated on the approach of death.

IV. THE DEATH OF THE EGO: MAGICAL MASTERY

The religiosity of older men helps them manage their chronic masculine concerns around power and production, though now within the passive voice. But it also contains expressions of an archaic coping style that normally makes its appearance—except among neurotics and psychotics—only in later life. This is the mode of *magical mastery*. It is distinguished from the preceding mastery positions by a lack of reality orientation. As we have seen, younger *active mastery* men have an "appetite for reality,"

[5] Erik Erikson, *Childhood and Society* (2nd edition), New York (Norton, 1963).

however abrasive that reality may be. They confront and are excited by challenges that they have created for themselves, by virtue of their own boldness. And while older men, in the passive mastery stage, tend to back away from the slings and arrows of the world, they still recognize that these exist. In both these orientations, the world and the self are surveyed fairly realistically; it is mainly the definitions of problem and of remedy that vary across the active and the passive positions. But in magical mastery, problems *per se* are either denied or responsibility for them is projected away from the self.[6]

Central to this stage is an erosion of ego boundaries, of the persisting sense of self/other distinctions. In effect, the world becomes a picture of what the subject fears or wants from the world; the usually persistent boundary placed between the province of the self and the domain of the other becomes unfixed, indeterminate, such that internal content of the self is mingled with and *perceived in* those external agents that pertain to those contents.

Seemingly, the boundaries that the ego normally maintains— though at a high cost in energy—are the outer aspects of the inner repressions and delaying mechanisms on which active mastery and instrumentality are founded. Once the active, instrumental phase of life is past, ego energy can be withdrawn from both the inner and the outer boundaries, and infantile demands for pleasure and security can flood back into the domains that they had previously held in early life. As they move back into skin, mouth, and sphincter the result is the turn towards diffuse sensuality that we noted earlier; and when they come to dominate

---

[6] In this stage, real threats can be summarily defined as blessings; an old Mayan looks at a TAT picture of malignant flying creatures hovering over a recumbent man, and declares that they are angels, come to bless and nourish a tired man. In his story the malignant birds that could stimulate his fear are transformed into "angels." The frightening beasts are in effect transformed into the comforting presence that an old man looks for when he is confronted by frightening beasts. This is magical mastery: the immediate, unboundaried, "umbilical" relationship between the stimulus, the subjective reaction that the stimulus provokes, and the final interpretation of the stimulus.

—as in childhood—the process of cognition and perception, the result is the stage of magical mastery.

Magical Mastery and Religion

This weakening of ego boundaries that is intrinsic to magical mastery is also integral to the rather vague, mystical religiosity of later life. The mystical experience, the sense that one is blended into some larger order of the universe, is predicated directly on the weakening of ego boundaries. For younger men whose ego boundaries are normally intact, the experience of mystical union, Freud's "oceanic sense," is artificially achieved through rhythmic chanting, through dancing, through identification with hypnotic leaders, or through drugs. In later life, as ego boundaries fray out and become "porous," the mystical sense of union with some divine order arises naturally.

Magical Mastery and Death

But magical mastery, for all that it is "regressive," and a recapitulation of early developmental stages, has a strange utility: it is the engine of the final phase of life. It appears to close the circle, to lead men naturally towards death. In magical mastery, as the boundaries of the self unravel, there takes place a kind of death of the ego which precedes the final death of the body. In order to avoid the horror of their end, men revive—through memory, through identification with children, through child-like behavior, through the taste of the foods that were first fed to them by their mothers—the weather of their beginning.[7] They thereby,

---

[7] Shortly before his death in 1965, the American poet Randall Jarrell wrote "Thinking of the Lost World," in which there is clearly expressed the wish to relive the beginning of life, with food being the touch-stone that calls up the climate of early life and mother's presence.

"This spoonful of chocolate tapioca
Tastes like peanut butter, like the vanilla
Extract mama told me not to drink.
Swallowing the spoonful, I have already travelled
Through time to my childhood. It puzzles me
That age is like it."

(From "The Lost World," by Randall Jarrell, New York: Collier, 1966.)

ly do not sleep more than five hours a
nd their extremities become cold and
el death creeping up their limbs. The
little deaths through action: they rise
ock, the sheepskin, and they go out—to
e case, to clear fields in the Mayan case,
ajo case.

are prone to the same passive yearnings
they also experience the temptation to
get out of the rat race, to consume rather
mit rather than to fight. The difference
l aged accept these urgings, the survivors,
, define them as a threat, and put them-
their own emergent passivity.

ually enjoy much social prestige, and this
h the pressures and the rewards for con-
are also aided in their final struggle
eir earliest identifications. Thus, where
to revive their identification with their
e of themselves as needful children), the
ely to maintain their identification with
taught them to work, to endure, and to
ive alternatives.[11]

jo would typically tell us about their hardihood train-
y were five or six years old, their father or uncle would
m sheepskin and toss them semi-naked into the snow
. "Now you must run a foot-race in the snow, down to
s you run. When you get to the spring you must break
ce. When you get back here you must go to that tree
he branches over yourself." We assumed that our sub-
evance over this treatment, but they claimed not to
cle said to me, 'I ran like this all my life, starting from
, you see that I have lived a long time, but my hair i
e the old-age lines in my face. This is because of tha
ade me tough. If you do this, you will live to be a
t; I did as he said, and I have lived a long time."
nces, the Navajo survivors were of course remindin
hardy youth. But these memories are functional as wel
the Navajo survivors remind themselves that, as in th

in the magical sense, deny death, deny the end; but the price is the "death" of the ego. The ego is dissipated, killed off because it will not finally relinquish the awareness of reality, including the awareness of oncoming death; and that act of murder—even though undertaken to preserve the illusion of rebirth and new beginnings—may set the stage for the final death of the body.[8]

These may sound like the mystical speculations of an investigator who has himself given way to magical mastery. But the sequence, magical mastery then physical death, shapes hard data. Lieberman's [9] reviews of psychological data from residents of an old persons' home who died medically unpredicted deaths show that their sudden decease was preceded by an equally sudden breakdown of ego functions towards magical mastery. Riegel's careful work makes a similar point: intellectual functioning does not decline across the adult years; rather, most forms of thinking hold steady across the adult life span, and only decline sharply and suddenly shortly before actual death.[10] Along similar lines, a comparison TAT of records given to me by the same Navajo subjects over a four-year period indicates that the intra-individual movement towards passive and magical imagery is greater for each successive age group, such that 40-year-old men show little shift in the regressive direction after four years, while 60-year-olds show a great deal. Thus, the degree of psychic regression appears to accelerate with nearness to death.

Narcissism and the Wish for Death

But the old man's relation to death includes more than fear and magical denial. There is also resignation, and beyond that

8 Along these lines, a crippled, 79-year-old Druze, whose wife has died recently, says that at the age of 80 he will "turn into a garden of flowers." I laugh with him about this, and suggest that he will become every kind of flower in the world; and fruits, as well. But this strong old man will not finally permit the murder of his ego. He leaves off laughing, and says, "But this is not true. We do not become flowers. This is a penicillin to ease pain." (What pain?) "The pain of death."

9 M. Lieberman and A. Coplan, "Distance from Death as a Variable in the Study of Aging," Developmental Psychology, 2, No. 1 (1969), pp. 71–84.

10 Personal communication from Dr. Klaus Riegel.

a welcoming of death. Thus, trans-culturally, men dream of death as an assassin, as an angry beast, as a canyon into which they fall; but they also dream of it and portray it in their projective test responses as a welcoming mother, or as a wide ocean in which they would like to swim. Some Druze men speak of this attraction for death with a passive voice: death is to be welcomed as an expression of God's will—to argue with death is to argue with God. Others speak of moving actively towards death, of forcing its hand: a 75-year-old Druze tells me: "I should die now, when I am at the height of my wisdom and strength and not when I have become weak and stupid, and children laugh at me in the streets." These instances may represent distinct ways of dealing with the inevitable; but they may also be rationalizations, whether expressed in obedient or defiant terms, of the wish for death.

But, if the old man's fear of death is so great that he relies on magical mastery to deny it, then why might he also seek death? This paradox is perhaps resolved if we consider some effects of narcissism, particularly the normal but also fairly pronounced narcissism of later life. In the narcissistic phase of relationships, the self is taken not only as the object of love, but of the full range of ambivalent feelings that are normally turned outwards, towards others: the self becomes the target of its own hate as well as of its own love. Where we love, we also hate, whether the object of our love is some other, or ourselves. Accordingly, when infantile narcissism is revived in later life, we can expect the self to be alternately exalted and diminished. Accordingly, we find that in later life the claims of the self for immediate satisfaction are raised above competing claims of others, of society, and of the reality principle itself; but by the same token, the same self is humbled before men and the gods, and death, the final extinction of the self, is also welcomed. Old men dream of assassins; but the murderer they fear is not only in their aging cells, it is in their own impulses, in the dark side of their own self-love.

If th
masculi
out-ride
the mor
and the
and/or
group, t
longitudi
this prop
sub-samp
logic bein
work, inac
be though
from deatl
life-span.
we should
preliterate
resources.
our sample
(55–69 year
dependency,
tiveness, and
as an extern

Their diff
striking: I h
to their corn
but because
corn. At wh
token ways—
Physical move
men. Inactivi
Navajo men c
up horseback r

---

the longevous men usual
night; more than that,
numb. It is as if they f
old survivors fight these
from the bed, the hamm
visit friends in the Druz
to herd sheep in the Na

These longevous men
as the "normal" aged;
relax, to take it easy, to
than to produce, to sub
is that where the norma
much like younger men
selves in opposition to

The old survivors us
provides them with bo
tinued activity. The
against passivity by th
the normal aged seem
mothers (and the sen
survivors are more li
the father figures who
choose active over pas

11 Thus, the survivor Nava
ing in early life. When the
drag them out of their war
outside of the hogan, saying
the spring. You must sing a
the ice and bring back a pi
and shake the snow from t
jects would retain some g
"It was done in love. My u
when I was real small. No
still black, and I do not ha
running in the snow. It
old as me.' And he was rig

Through these reminis
themselves and us of their
as expressive: through the

Survival and the Need For An Enemy

Thus, old survivors still maintain the combative, resistant, *stubborn* posture: they mainly turn it inwards, against their own "weakness," but they still turn it outwards, towards challenge from impersonal nature, or from human enemies. I rarely talk to such a man, in any culture, without finding that he is embroiled in a struggle with some real or imagined enemy. For the longevous Navajo, the enemy is likely to be some witch "way over there," who is jealous of their wealth and is making lethal spells against them; and among the Druze the enemy is some neighbor presumably encroaching on their lands. Even where life does not offer evidence of real enemies, old survivors are likely to imagine them and to turn bucolic and potentially peaceful activities into fantasy wars. Thus, I ask a 100-year-old Navajo found planting, why corn is still so important to him, and he replies: "You must understand that corn is like your wife, and the weeds are like another man who comes to steal your wife. You have to kill those weeds!" Unlike the pre-survivor aged men, this veteran does not dwell on the beauty or the taste of the corn; rather, he reverses the usual age priorities and turns a potentially oral experience into an occasion of rivalry and combat.

In sum, the normal aged seem to use magical mastery in the form of gross *denial* of reality in order to protect their passivity: "I do not have to act; someone up there loves me, and everything is for the best in the best of all possible worlds." By contrast, the old survivors use magical mastery in the form of *projective* distortions of reality in order to justify their continued action: "There is a sea of troubles, of enemies, and I must take arms up against them." They turn the death within their bodies into a thief or into an assassin "out there" who can be fought, and by thus externalizing and personalizing their enemy they preserve the active, fighting stance on which continued life may partly depend.

---

past, continued survival is *still* guaranteed by continued movement, by rejection of tempting beds, the warm sheepskin, the recumbent, passive position.

I have spoken to many doctors about this matter, and all of them admit that death can be predicted, in the absence of "hard" clinical data, when the patient "stops fighting." Working from the other end of the life-cycle, the psychoanalyst Ernst Kris has shown that foundling infants under "adequate" though impersonal care will develop a depressive apathetic "hospitalism" syndrome that is notably lethal to them. By the same token, longitudinal studies of our panel of traditional Navajo indicate that men who score high on the various indices of passive-dependency at time 1 are much more likely than men with low scores on this dimension to develop severe and/or terminal diseases by time 2, four years later. This effect is predictable, regardless of age, except for the very oldest men. All these convergent findings, from a wide range of populations, suggest that there may be something quite deadly about the passive-dependent conformation. Conversely, there may be something life-preserving about the stubborn, recalcitrant posture. Sweet, wise old men deserve better, but they seem to be losers. Perhaps the fighting, oppositional stance is the psychic counterpart of a generally more vital organism; or perhaps this oppositional stance itself keeps the organism tuned up to such a pitch that it can better overcome disease effects. If so, then in later life the necessary mobilization is brought about by a kind of "adaptive paranoia" that provides the fighting survivor with the necessary but non-existent enemies that he requires to keep him on his toes.[12] The old curmudgeons do finally die, but it is usually under protest: they "do not go gentle into that good-night."

Perhaps we can summarize the findings and speculations concerning longevity and survival with this observation: The men who die before age 70 in traditional societies go to death as to

[12] Women are much more likely than men to rely on adaptive paranoia in later life. For them, this defense sponsors much intrusive and offensive behavior. It permits old women to interfere in the lives of others, "for their own good." Consequently, they remain fighters; and perhaps this is why old women typically outlive milder, gentler husbands.

a mother; and those survivors who live beyond seventy fight it like a father.[13]

VI. PRE-SENILE YOUTH: THE COUNTER-CULTURE

I have described two postures, two syndromes, found among aging men. One involves disavowal of aggression and competition, and their replacement by dependency, sensuality and ego diffusion. It is associated with early death, or with a life span of less than 70 years. The contrast syndrome is centered mainly around aggression and resistance against passive-dependent wishes within the self, and against those outer agents that would force the self into a passive and dependent position. This active assertive orientation is associated with temporal distance from death, and with survival, being mainly found among the younger men of our samples, those far from death, or among the very old men, who have outlived most of their fellows. Turning back to the topic of youthful involvement with death, we can see that the so-called counter-culture has amplified and made a politics out of the first complex of attitudes—those associated with normal aging, with closeness to death, and with low survival. The counter-culture, its theorists and PR men have co-opted, as the very badge of youth and renewal, those qualities which are the species insignia of aging.[14]

[13] The mountaineer tribesmen of the Caucasus are famous for their longevity. They are quite explicit about the "paternal" nature of the death that they fight. Thus, a ninety-year-old horseman meeting his crony on the road will say, "I've beaten the old man for another year."

[14] I cannot be very specific as to what I mean by the counter-culture. (Substitute "Hippies" if you need a more concrete referent, but the boundaries of that group have also become very blurred.) I am referring to that admittedly amorphous, always changing cohort, mostly young, composed of all those who live in opposition to an official "establishment" culture which reputedly emphasizes the values of competition, industry and the consumption of mass-produced goods. I exempt the activist radicals: these reject the official culture, but they also reject the more self-indulgent, pleasure-oriented aspects of the counter-culture—such as hard drugs.

Counter-Aggression and Counter-Productivity in the Counter-Culture

Consider for example the pivotal matter of aggression, which is repudiated both by aging men and by the "kids"—and for much the same reason, namely, that individual aggression is disruptive to community, to oneness with others. Thus, many young people now react to a competitive urge within themselves as their puritan ancestors might have reacted to an impulse towards illicit sex. And their major charge against the university, one most likely to fuel their rebellion, is that it forces them—through grading systems, exams and other occasions of sin [15]—to compete against each other.

Perhaps as part of the turn away from competition, the counter-culture also sponsors the same turn away from productivity that we find among aging men of various cultures. Of course, certain forms of productivity are still extolled by the counter-culture: the production of handicrafts, or organic foods, etc. However, there is at the same time a rejection of *apprenticeship*. Thus, any production which reflects untutored spontaneous "creativity" is encouraged; but the process of education for production, which involves delaying the pleasure of self-expression, and the acceptance of standards which have not been devised by the self, is generally discredited.

The Sponsorship of Dependency in the Counter-Culture

The management of dependency is also similar among the young men of the counter-culture and aging men in general.

---

[15] I would have more sympathy for this position if it were really possible to legislate aggression out of existence by a kind of *fiat* of the liberal will. But aggression denied, or deprived of its usual occasions does not disappear; it only defines new goals. I once observed an encounter group where the participants were told to line up according to their importance in the group. Four young men—but no girls—shoved and contended against each other for five minutes for the last place in line; and they only left off when the dominance "lower-archy" had finally been established.

True, the counter-culture does not espouse dependency as openly as it supports non-violence and counter-dominance. The dependent aged can plead a life of service to others, but the alienated young lack this justification, and so do not voice their succorant wishes as openly as their elders. However, such needs are central to both cohorts. While they are not openly avowed, the dependent wishes are lived out by young men (and women) in explicit ways, particularly in regard to emotional supplies. David Riesman wrote twenty years ago of the other-directed quality of American youth, who rely on their peer groups and peer group leaders for legitimation, identity and direction. Where the old man might see his physical existence threatened without the protection of some strong provider, many young people feel that their psychic existence is threatened unless it is validated by the immediate tangible presence of their peers, those who are most like themselves. The "lonely crowd" has become the lonely T-Group, and it is particularly in such quasi-communities, the encounter and the T-Groups, that the demands for love and complete acceptance that Riesman could only infer twenty years ago are now directly voiced. Furthermore, the demands have escalated: words are no longer sufficient to convey the message of acceptance and love. More and more the demand is for some token of the immediate, physical presence of the other—the touch, the reassuring caress, regardless of whether it is given by man or woman, friend or stranger.

And, like the aged, who worship in some external form the power and resource that they can no longer feel within themselves, important segments of youth—whether the New Left, the Jesus freaks, or the addicts of rock—pay homage to their particular human icons: the "charismatic" rock stars, drug cult leaders, movement heavies, encounter group papalois, commune tyrants, or revolutionary *enragés*. Anybody who can speak with authority, who has some supplies of his own, who does not seem to care if he is loved, can quickly become a center of adoration by those sad, empty, strangely "uninflated" children who throng the urban world today. The politics of the hero do not really matter: Left or Right, racist or universalist, John Wayne and Eldridge Cleaver are both admired more than any well-meaning but undramatic liberal.

The Sponsorship of Sensuality in the Counter-Culture

But, as with the aged, the receptive orientation involves supplies from non-human as well as human sources. We have described the "post-genital" sensuality of the aging man, the mild pleasure that he takes in the rediscovered pleasures of mouth, sphincters and eyes. Similar pleasure strivings mark the young food-faddists of the counter-culture, who share with the aged the interesting belief that they *are* what they *eat*. Thus, inner purity can be guaranteed by organically grown foods. Like the rock superstar, organic food is another "hero" of the counter-culture: it is an external source of strength and wholeness to be absorbed into the self, whether through identification, imitation, or mastication. And as with the aged, what is taken in through these means becomes the core of the superego: good food means more than good flavor—it is the assurance of inner spiritual goodness, as well.

Food is not only moral for this segment of youth; it is also loved. Oral imagery is found everywhere in their culture, from the names of rock groups, (The Cream, The Lovin' Spoonful, The Carnal Kitchen), to the titles of favored books, (*Watermelon Sugar, The Naked Lunch, The Strawberry Statement*). There is an obsessive concern with oral tranquilizers, particularly sweet wine and marijuana.

The visual interests common among old men are also important to the young: light shows, posters, hallucinations, movies. And the addiction to flicks is so extreme that movie-makers now cater almost exclusively to the youth market.[16]

---

[16] The concentration on oral and visual intake is shown in an account of the

Similarly, photography has become a leading hobby for the green Americans: the most expensive Nikons and their armory of special lenses dangle and shine between scruffy beards and ragged jeans. By the same token, every rock group has its attendant *paparazzi*, whose hand-held cameras photograph the action generated in the swarm by the very presence of a hand-held camera.

Regarding this matter of diffuse sensuality, the parallels between the aged and the counter-culturists could be drawn out indefinitely. To sum up, in both cohorts we see the withdrawal from genital sexuality towards a mild sensuality that is no longer restricted to a few erogenous zones, but is diffused over all sense organs, sphincters, and skin surfaces. In the aged the pleasures of the table tend to replace the sharper but briefer and often more troublesome ecstasies of the bed; and in the young cohort we also see that—despite all the public relations of the "sexual revolution"—there is a devaluation of genital sex in favor of diffuse pleasure experience. In the young this shift has some political and ideological back-up. For one thing, women's lib functions as an Orwellian Anti-Sex League: young men are instructed to feel guilty about the sexual desires that presumably reduce their lady-friends to the status of "objects." Then too, the aging movement gurus, Norman O. Brown and Herbert Marcuse, have pushed the idea that polymorphous sensuality, normal in later life, represents "liberation" and "life-enhancement" for all ages. The libidinal position that old men *must* adopt is presented to young men as the one that they *should* prefer over the other options that are available to them.

life-style established by Michael Wilding, 19-year-old son of Elizabeth Taylor, after he dropped out of the $80,000 London home that his mother had given to him as a wedding present. The "young man has now settled in a farmhouse in the Cambrian Mountains to live frugally with a commune 'family.' They are living on organically-grown grain and tea made with goat's milk, forswearing all luxuries except a color television set." (From the European edition of the *Herald Tribune*, May 2, 1972.)

The Sponsorship of Unisex by the Counter-Culture

Politics and propaganda cannot be the sole, independent signs of the profound contemporary shifts in sexual styles. The rhetoric of unisex and polymorphous sexuality could only come along after the fact to legitimize the deep shifts away from the phallic orientation that had already taken place among the young. The point is, while the various elements of the counter-culture are justified separately on ideological grounds, our review of the life-style of the aging, which contains similar elements, suggests that these seemingly disparate elements may be equivalent expressions of an over-all syndrome which integrates them all. They are all parts of an overriding and recurrent pattern in which one aspect tends to predict the presence of the others.

Thus, the anti-phallic emphasis is related to another point of resemblance between the aged and present-day youth: the loss of inter-sexual distinctions, and the merging of men and women towards *unisex*. As we have seen, this routinely comes about in later life, when each sex can afford to live out some of the potentials, passive or aggressive, that had been denied to them in the service of the parental role. Their previous self-denial has earned the aged the right to consume life-styles that were previously out of bounds to them. The young seem now to be demanding the same consumer's right, though without having first paid the usual dues: the right to be psychopathic and sensitive, active and passive, hard and soft, man and woman—all of the above, and all at once. In any event, it is clear that young men are busily exploring the hitherto closed-off possibilities of sensitivity, adorn-ment, tenderness, and receptive sex; while girls, eschewing cos-metics, are everywhere hiking out on their various visionary quests, intent on proving their manhood. Thus, the usual pattern of late middle life, the tough, domineering wife linked to sweet but vague grandpa, has become the pattern of the young unisex couple. As Thurber described them, "She, bold as a hawk; he, soft as the doe." [17]

The Religiosity of the Counter-Culture

We have mentioned the religiosity of the aged. The parallels among youth are again clear, and were evident even before the advent of the Jesus freaks. Prior to them, the young had mainly gravitated to varieties of Eastern mysticism, laced with food-cultism; and these directions had been pioneered for them by dotty old ladies in California. As with the aged, the religiosity of the young has in it the desire to lose a weak self and to merge with some larger entity that betokens strength, wholeness, and productivity. The old turn to these sources because the internal order upon which their own productivity is based is being disassembled, deprived of sustaining energy; but the young of our urban world turn towards divine representations of strength and life because (although they are bright and "creative") they have never developed the sense of internal resource in the first place. They do not seem to find the models, the experiences, the disciplines which could leave them with an accrued sense of *internal* resource. They do not develop the sense that, all by themselves, they have what they need to survive. They are therefore often unable to make the basic shift, pivotal to maturation, from trusting the resources of the supportive other to trusting the resources of the self. Lacking this self-reliance they remain endlessly dependent on various versions of the strong and relia-

[17] The shift towards early unisex is partly a product of feminism, but it also stimulates the latest forms of women's lib. The fact is, that as men explore the receptive aspect of their nature, they also become more exploitative, more inclined to take, without giving much back except their charm. They become towards their girl-friends as Victorian women once were towards "responsible" men: exploiting, manipulative, demanding and "cute." Victorian men could put up with this as the price of their superior masculine prestige. And now that women in their turn have to put up with hysteroid men, they are demanding an equivalent pay-off in prestige.

ble other: the group, the "people," the charismatic leader, or—
like the aged—the omnipotent gods.

The Cult of Madness, and the Hatred of the Ego

Finally, the two cohorts, the normal aged and the counter-
culture youth, have in common the rage against the ego. For the
ego is both the creation of self-boundaries, and their creator; and
ego boundaries stand in the way of the desired experience of
merging, of union with something larger and more powerful
than the self. The hatred of the ego is intense and explicit in
the counter-culture, whether it is expressed as the distrust of
rationality, the intolerance of delay, or the impatience with
linear thinking. The complaint among contemporary students—
even graduate students—is that their acquired habits of rationality and categorical thinking cut them off from *union* with the
phenomenon or group that they are asked to consider. As one
student in my field-work class put it, "I don't want to *study* the
community, I want to be *part* of it!" And this middle-class
Jewish student went on to explain that only the exercise of his
intellect put a boundary between himself and the "people" (in
this case, inner-city blacks).

A more ominous symptom of the rage against the ego is the
cult of madness, the contemporary adulation, *a la* R. D. Laing, of
the psychotic. The current youthful sentimentality about mad-
men is based on a naive Rousseauism of the inner life, on the
belief that there is within the deepest recesses of the self some
inner strength, perfection, wholeness already formed and waiting
for release. Inner resources are not *potentials* to be brought
into being through hard work, they are *already there* waiting
for the magic touchstone that will unlock the prison that the ego
has set about them. For the ego is the villain in this drama:
just as the young accuse their own ego of cutting them off
from external centers of love and wholeness, so do they accuse
it of blocking access to some inner treasury of spontaneity, crea-

tivity and perfection. On both counts the ego is suspect, to be abolished.[18] Madness, as the death of the ego, is coded as liberation, creativity, *life*.

For the aged, the antagonism towards the ego, and the passage into magical mastery is accomplished fairly easily: it is a side effect of the draining away of vital energy from the structures of the ego. But in youth the ego does not die easily. It has to be overcome by acts of "revolutionary" violence: drugs, particularly the hallucinogenics, are the Molotov cocktails which accomplish the internal revolution against the ego. They bring about the unboundaried state which is achieved naturally in later life. The counter-culture drugs are a kind of pre-senility equivalent; anybody who has seen a geriatric ward and a pot party can recognize their essential sameness. Thus, Woodstock was not peaceful because our youth has by some magic learned to love; it was peaceful because of marijuana, which turned the young participants into replicas of their grandparents in, say, St. Petersburg, Florida: nodding, dozing, and beaming in the sun.

Encounter groups, implosive therapy, group-grope, rock music, are also "plastiques" in the warfare against the ego. Where drugs are mainly levelled against the internal id-ego boundary, the various group techniques are designed to reduce the outer, self/other boundaries. They are in the service of a kind of "socialism of affluence" which aims to collectivize experience, rather than capital goods. In the group setting, for a while at least, the inner contents of the psyche and the flesh that covers it become pooled, defined as collective property. In the Esalen-style settings there is practiced a kind of id-communism where distinctions between inner and outer, between self and other, between group and individual are treated with the same disdain as traditional

18 Any true clinician knows that this modern appreciation of schizophrenia is in truth a form of necrophilia masquerading as the celebration of life. For schizophrenia is psychic *death*—the death of community, and of the self that lives in and through community. And the schizophrenic who howls in the night is not celebrating his liberation from community; he is experiencing the horror of these deaths, and of utter aloneness.

Marxists treat the distinction between state and private property. But this revolution is against the individual, not the state; and the goal is to bring about the dissolution of the self-boundary and the triumph of magical mastery that is the normal state of affairs at the end of the life-cycle. For both cohorts, old and young, the ego is sacrificed in order to reinstate the early illusion of omnipotence, the consoling "oceanic" sense that one includes or is included in everything that is strong and whole in the universe.

Here again is the paradox of narcissism: we cannot make the self the center of and target of our love without also making it the center and target of our lethal hate; and we cannot exalt the self and restore its original infantile claims without destroying whatever is most distinctive and individual about the self. That the destruction of ego is touted to us by Charles Reich as Consciousness III, or the "discovery of self," does not change matters. The sentimental myth that drives such thinking is that loss or destruction of intra- and inter-individual boundaries is necessary for freedom and for the expansion of self-consciousness. In reality, at least in regard to aging, it is the condition that seems to precede somatic death. For other age-groups it may lead to morbid preoccupations with death, and to rather suicidal flirtations with death—as through hard drug use—of the sort that are becoming terribly popular now. And on the political level the dissolution of the ego is the precondition for the kind of social death that we call totalitarianism. Like the gods or like the charismatic cult-leaders, the totalitarian leader claims that perfection and wholeness reside only in him, and that followers can be included in his perfection and power if they will give up their *boundaries,* the prides and distinctions that go into defining their ego and their individuality. Like it or not, for all the isolations and alienations that it imposes, for all that it reminds us of the deaths and the obligations that we want to forget, the ego and its supporting institutions are the best guarantors of individual liberty that we have. In a real world there is nothing else.

VII. ANTI-INSTRUMENTALISM: CAUSES AND CONSEQUENCES

My personal biases against the counter-culture, and against normal aging come through clearly in this paper. This is because I am afraid of both of them, and probably for much the same reasons. Thus, I study aging because I am afraid of it. This is my particular piece of magical mastery: the particular illusion that drives my research is that it *is not* my job to become that which it *is* my job to study. To put it in a more flattering way, I am against death—for others as well as for myself. My fear of the counter-culture has the same root as my fear of age. Both represent to me a kind of death—the death of the body in the one case, and the death of the ego in the other. And like the old traditional Navajo, I respond to the kind of passivity that the counter-culture publicizes and politicizes as though it were a metaphor of death. Admittedly, my own subjective linking of death with passivity may lead me to see similarities between the psychology of the pre-morbid aged and the counter-culture youth that exist only in my own head. Possibly so. But while my bias no doubt leads to various distortions, I do not think that it led me to see connections that were not there; rather, I think that it made me particularly sensitive to some more than super-ficial resemblances between "new" youth and the aged that have to do with their relationship to the productive life.[19]

[19] I am not the first observer to note the similarity between the post-pubescent and the pre-senescent. Saul Alinsky, the well-known community organizer, notes the anti-instrumentality of large segments of this generation, and likens it to old age: "I've run into more senility among the 19 to 20-year-olds than among the aged . . . life is too much for them, so they jump off into a mystical future . . . These kids are not going for a revolution, they are going for a revelation" . . . He advised a college audience to stop looking for somebody with charisma, and to get busy and start organizing . . . "Do you want to communicate, or sit there like God?" (New York *Times,* Jan. 5, 1971.)

Dr. James Anthony, a psychoanalyst, draws the psychological parallels between

The point is that both older men and the young men of the counter-culture share a common stance towards the productive, achieving life that perhaps accounts for the similarities in ego structure and function that have been outlined here. True, the aged men are *post-productive,* while the new young have remained in the *pre-productive* position; but both cohorts have turned against the instrumental life, and the psychological consequences of that rejection are much the same in each case. Men who reject instrumentality may do so in the name of liberation, but they have bound themselves to consequences which are as predictable and as fixed as those which are contingent on the opposite choice of a hard-working and competitive existence: namely, diffuse sensuality, unisex, reliance on illusion, vague religiosity, and all the rest of the package.

Thus, it appears to me that aging, in the sense that I have been discussing it, is not limited to a particular period of life. Among men, psychological aging occurs whenever the productive, autonomous position is either abandoned or fails to develop. In this fundamental respect, the normal aged and the alienated young men are alike. What differentiates the old from the young are their reasons for turning away from instrumentality. The old man has outgrown the period of chronic emergency that required his focussed instrumentality. Weakened by age and effort, his species and social dues paid, he can repossess some of the pleasures that he was once coaxed and socialized into giving up. The instrumental life is difficult at best, most men do not really like it, they take it up grudgingly, and they only accept it in exchange for much symbolic reward of status and prestige. Accordingly, aging men retire from the active, instrumental life quickly enough and

youth and age in a more systematic way. He claims that present-day adolescents, far more often than their predecessors, show symptoms of aging even before they are out of their teens. He claims that oldsters' and adolescents' most commonly shared symptom is depression: "For both the future looks black and unappealing . . . *Preoccupation with death and nothingness is frequent.*" Besides, the two groups are alike in being "intensely self-absorbed; the narcissism of old age and the narcissism of adolescence are two peaks in the development of human egotism." (Reported in *Time,* May 1, 1972.)

with some relief when their productivity in the material sense is no longer required and when their prestige can rest on other bases, such as participation in the religious life of their community.[20]

The aged of traditional societies drop out of the productive system when they have an organized moral system that they can at the same time drop *into*. The problem is different for alienated youth who refuse, even from the start, to affiliate with the technical-productive order of the secular society. Erik Erikson (*op. cit.*) once wrote that deprivation is not in itself bad; it is only deprivation without meaning that is personally destructive. The point is that secular, urbanized society, with all its sponsorship of scepticism and irreverence, eventually leads its most talented youth to question the legitimacy of its institutions and of the symbolic rewards that these can bestow. Once institutions and authorities lose legitimacy, they lose the power to provide *meaningful* symbolic rewards in exchange for the deprivations that they require in the service of combat or productivity. The possible trade-off between deprivation and meaning ceases to exist as an option for young men, and with it goes much of the basis for the productive orientation. Thus, the complex, secular society does not have the power possessed by the simplest, most backward folk society to create legitimacy, or to sanctify the upper reaches of its status hierarchies. In the secular urbanized society, the badge of rank, the medal for valor, the membership in the honorary society cease to be rewards that men are ready to fight, die or sweat for. Thus, strangely enough, as society becomes more

[20] In traditional societies the aged do not, as Cumming and Henry claim, disengage themselves from the normative control systems of their society; rather, they switch their allegiance from the systems of normative control that regulate productivity to those based on the moral and religious requirements of their society. They cease to be productive agents in their own right, and they take up the task of maintaining the community's contact with the productive powers of the supernatural. The great virtue of traditional society for the aged is that within it they can live out the passive-receptive side of their natures without finally losing touch with some beneficent, productive order of the universe. See E. Cumming and W. E. Henry, *Growing Old: The Study of Disengagement*, New York (Basic Books, 1961).

complex, its component individuals tend to become—psychologically at least—more primitive. Unwilling to settle for more abstract and intangible rewards, for tokens of honor and prowess, they demand in exchange for their effort more immediate, tangible enjoyments: material goods, sex, drugs, sounds, textures, foods, *experiences*—and preferably all of them at once. The secular society becomes the consumer society, and finally for any chronological age, the *geriatric* society. Cut off from meaningful work by mass production, by the absence of clear necessities, and by the failure of symbolic incentives, the young men spiral slowly towards the psychological conditions normal for the aged: they become a premature gerontocracy. Perhaps that is why the young are fascinated with death; though chronologically they stand at the beginning of life, psychologically many of them live close, too close, to the end. And as we see from the rising number of stupid, useless deaths and cripplings from drugs, VD, and suicide, many are tempted—with the impulsivity of youth—to hurry to that end.

DEATH AND THE NATIVE STRAIN
IN AMERICAN POETRY

BY HAROLD BLOOM

Shall we be found hanging in the trees next spring?
Of what disaster is this the imminence:
Bare limbs, bare trees and a wind as sharp as salt?

The stars are putting on their glittering belts,
They throw around their shoulders cloaks that flash
Like a great shadow's last embellishment.

It may come tomorrow in the simplest word,
Almost as part of innocence, almost,
Almost as the tenderest and the truest part.

THIS is Wallace Stevens in expectation of an imminent death. The context is the American Sublime; the poem is his masterpiece, *The Auroras of Autumn.* When the poem attains its resolution, the auroras cease to be a spell of light or false sign of heavenly malice, and are seen as an innocence of the earth. Death, which may come tomorrow, is not called part of that innocence, but *almost* part of it—even almost what it is in Whitman, the tenderest and truest part of innocence. Whitman and Stevens, both central to American poetic tradition, are wholly at the American imaginative center in their visions of death. Mortality, when confronted by the native strain in our poetry, is neither religiously denied nor transformed into something strangely rich. Death is part of the family, and its enigma is assimilated to the mystery of origins, where it is granted the true priority.

I want to contrast the visions of death in British and American poetry, and though I will take my instances of both free-style, I will keep coming back to a central poet of each tradition and a central text of death in each poet. Yeats and Stevens are inevitable contraries, being the largest heirs, respectively, of British and American Romanticism. I want two mysterious, hieratic poems, pre-elegies for the poet's own death, and out of a number of possibilities I choose Yeats' *Cuchulain Comforted* and Stevens' *The Owl in the Sarcophagus.* Yet to apprehend these poems we need to know other poems by Yeats and Stevens, and the inescapable poems of their precursors: Blake, Shelley, Keats and Browning for Yeats; these same poets, but also the American line of Emerson, Whitman, and Dickinson for Stevens. This discussion, then, attempts to illuminate Yeats by his ancestors and by his contrary, Stevens, and also to see through Stevens and his American ancestry a peculiarly national vision of death. Yeats, though esoteric, moves towards a broader European account (and acceptance) of death, but the American poetic story of death is less universal, and probably more of an evasion of death our death, an evasion that is the ultimate triumph of imaginative solipsism.

Blake and Emerson, two very different Romantic founding fathers, had a common disinterest in death, unlike their major disciples. Blake said he could not think that death was more than a going-out from one room into another, which is a dismissal we might expect from a consciousness strong enough to believe that "The ruins of Time build mansions in Eternity." Emerson, in his best essay, *Experience,* has resort to death as a final antidote to the illusoriness of all phenomena: "Nothing is left us now but death. We look to that with a grim satisfaction, saying, There at least is reality that will not dodge us." Yet this is Emerson in a fine exasperation with his (and our) own skepticism. More often, he is subtly dialectical in his devaluation of death. Aged thirty-nine, he writes in his journal, "The only poetic fact in the life of thousands and thousands is their death. No wonder they specify all the circumstances of the death of another person." At forty, he protests, "Now, if a man dies, it is like a grave dug in the snow, it is a ghastly fact abhorrent to Nature, and we never mention it. Death is as natural as life, and should be sweet and graceful." At the age of fifty-one, he sums up the strength of his wisdom, but with the resignation of the seer who doubts the communicability of his vision:

> A man of thought is willing to die, willing to live; I suppose because he has seen the thread on which the beads are strung, and perceived that it reaches up and down, existing quite independently of the present illusions. A man of affairs is afraid to die, is pestered with terrors, because he has not this vision. Yet the first cannot explain it to the second.

Emerson and Blake, who disagree on most things, including the relative goodness of the natural man, are nearly at one in their realization that death is not *materia poetica*. Wordsworth, the other prime founder of Romanticism in the poetry of our language, is much closer to all later Romantics in his poetic anxieties about death. Yeats, though consciously repelled by Wordsworth, followed after Wordsworth's imaginative patterns quite as much as Stevens did, and Stevens is an overt Wordsworthian. In this, Yeats and Stevens repeat the contrast between Shelley and Keats, both of whom developed Wordsworth's central arguments—but Shelley by opposing their naturalism and Keats by making such naturalism even more heroic.

Wordsworth fought the *consciousness* of death because he had begun by identifying the poetic spirit with the intimation of immortality. His means for fighting a self-consciousness so destructive was to beget again the glory of his youth by the pursuit and recapture of after-images, defined by Geoffrey Hartman as re-cognitions leading to recognitions. By entering again into the gleam of immortality, through recollected images, Wordsworth almost persuaded himself that he could renovate his consciousness so as to attain again the child's freedom from any sense of mortality.

Shelley, a skeptic yet a visionary, apprehended the Wordsworthian gleam as a constant inconstant, a flickering sense of what he called the Intellectual Beauty. Primarily an erotic poet, Shelley centered his concern on the shadow of ruin that haunted every manifestation of the Intellectual Beauty, particularly in heterosexual love, in all its glory and in its cyclic decay. Death, for Shelley, is essentially the absence or ruin of Eros. For Keats, with his faith in the senses, death is part of the body, and part therefore of Eros. Even as Keats is incapable of unperplexing joy from pain, so he discovers we cannot unperplex bodily love from death. It is—Keats sings—in the very temple of delight that veiled Melancholy has her solitary shrine. After the quester, Keats adds, proves capable of viewing this, he is capable only of a distinguished death: "to be among her cloudy trophies hung." As Hart Crane says of his idioms in one of his elegies, so we might say of Keats's questers: "They are no trophies of the sun." Like Stevens after him, Keats yields graciously to what Freud would call the Reality Principle. Yeats outrageously and splendidly would not so yield, and in this he had both English Romantic and Victorian precursors (Browning most powerfully), even as Stevens was schooled in yielding by the two best American Poets, Whitman and Dickinson.

Browning's triumph over the Reality Principle does not come through his vehement temperament, much impressed as we may be when he growls at us that he would no more fear death than he would any other battle. We are more moved when Childe Roland dauntless touches the slug-horn to his lips even as a horrible and nameless death closes upon him. But a kind of vehemence is involved in Childe Roland too, and I will return to Browning's magnificent invention when *Cuchulain Comforted* becomes the main text, for *Cuchulain Comforted* is Yeats' version of *Childe Roland to the Dark Tower Came*. Though Santayana attacked Browning and Whitman together as "poets of Barbarism," there is nothing in common between the two, including their clashing visions of death. This rapid induction to a contrast between British and American poetries of death can move to Yeats and Stevens by way of Whitman's contrast to Browning, with a side glance at Dickinson's severe originalities in this, her great subject.

Whitman, in the concluding sections of *Song of Myself*, meets death our death as being indistinguishable from an Orphic Eros, a release that is fulfillment:

> And as to you Death, and you bitter hug of mortality,
>   it is idle to try to alarm me.
>
> To his work without flinching the accoucheur comes,
> I see the elder-hand pressing receiving supporting,
> I recline by the sills of the exquisite flexible doors,
> And mark the outlet, and mark the relief and escape.

Here, as at the end of *The Sleepers*, neither we nor Whitman know precisely whether we are talking about a womb or a tomb, birth or death. Yet Whitman, unlike Browning or Yeats, is not concerned about personal immortality in the sense of an individual survival. "I shall clasp thee again," Browning insists, and in his last *Epilogue* reminds us he always "Held we fall to rise, are baffled to fight better,/Sleep to wake." Browning's is a highly individual, truly a private Protestantism, yet it is still Protestant, but Whitman's religion is American Orphism, which is a very different faith. Dickinson, who had in common with Whitman only Emerson as prime precursor, shares in this Orphism but with a very different emphasis, and an accent entirely her own creation.

Emerson was Orphic about everything except death, which may suggest he was more an Orphic speculator than an Orphic believer. He had fostered a faith that Whitman, Thoreau, and Dickinson all possessed, yet he entertained it more speculatively than they did. American Orphism, which seems to me still the religion of the ongoing native strain in our poetry, emphasizes not the potential divinity of man but the actual divinity already present in the creative spirit. Divination, in every sense of that term, is the enterprise of the native strain in American poetry. What Wordsworth hesitantly affirmed becomes literal doctrine in American Romanticism. The American Orphic not only worships the gods Bacchus, Eros, and Ananke or Necessity, as the ancient followers of Orpheus did, but he seeks to become those gods. Zeus, Apollo, Jehovah and Christ count for less in

American poetry than Bacchus, Eros and Ananke do, for the American Orpheus begins in the Evening-land, and so starts out in the belief that he is already a quasi-god, who perhaps can evade true death through divination, by joining gods like Dionysus, Eros, and Ananke, all of whom include death, and so surmount it.

Dickinson is too strong and too subtle to divinate without every kind of shading reservation. What matters in her is consciousness, and this is rarely so much consciousness of death as it is the consciousness of consciousness, even when it is death that is being apprehended:

> This Consciousness that is aware
> Of Neighbors and the Sun
> Will be the one aware of Death
> And that itself alone
>
> Is traversing the interval
> Experience between
> And most profound experiment
> Appointed unto Men—
>
> How adequate unto itself
> Its properties shall be
> Itself unto itself and none
> Shall make discovery.
>
> Adventure most unto itself
> The Soul condemned to be—
> Attended by a single Hound
> Its own identity.

A consciousness that she tells us is not solipsistic, since it is aware of other selves and of the external world, will some day be aware of dying, and will be altogether solitary, autonomous, and unable to communicate its final knowing to others. This final adventure will be a quest indistinguishable from the quester, and yet the quester will know herself as a shaman might, surviving so long as her totemic hound survives. This division between soul or character, and self or personality or identity is a distinction made in different ways in Browning, Whitman and Yeats, yet never as starkly as Dickinson conveys it. What matters in her is a heroism that says only consciousness matters. Death interests her as a challenge to consciousness, but not as a challenge to any other capacity for heroism.

Heroism meant nearly everything to Yeats; he overvalued violence because he was so desperate in his search for the heroic character. His central hero is the legendary Cuchulain, who inspired his finest verse-dramas, *At the Hawk's Well* and *The Only Jealousy of Emer*. Yeats's last play, left unrevised, is *The Death of Cuchulain*; his last poem-but-one is the majestic *Cuchulain Comforted*, as good a poem as ever he wrote. Yeats dated it 13 January 1939; on January 28 he died. Dorothy Wellesley, who heard Yeats read aloud a prose version of the poem, gives this as part of her memory of it: One of the shades speaks to Cuchulain, the just-slain hero:

> . . . you will like to know who we are. We are the people who run away from the battles. Some of us have been put to death as cowards, but others have hidden, and some even died without people knowing they were cowards . . .

In the poem, *Cuchulain Comforted*, the Shrouds tell Cuchulain their character: "Convicted cowards all, by kindred slain/Or driven from home and left to die in fear." They omit those who die, their cowardice still unknown by others. Cuchulain, "violent and famous," is the antithesis of a coward, and so is Browning's obsessive quester, Childe Roland, who nevertheless enters the after-life ringed by cowards and traitors, failed fellow-questers, just as Cuchulain does. Is Yeats, like Browning, struggling with an obscure sense of self-betrayal, of a moral cowardice he believes himself not to have expiated?

As Helen Vendler has noted, the beautiful close of *Cuchulain Comforted*, "They had changed their throats and had the throats of birds," echoes Dante's great vision of Brunetto Latini, who is in Hell, yet seems one of the victorious and not among the defeated. This is the accent of celebration and not of bitterness, and we can say therefore that Yeats, though equivocal, is not turning against the theme of heroism in this death-poem. The cowards are transfigured, even as Roland's failed companions are transfigured when they stand ranged about him as a living flame, as he sounds his last trumpet of a prophecy. The hero has joined the failures, blent into one final state where the antithesis between heroism and cowardice, success and failure, has broken down far more thoroughly, somehow, than the unbreakable antithesis between life and death.

Yeats compels us, in *Cuchulain Comforted* as in a surprising number of other poems, to a close knowledge of his system in *A Vision*. The weight of Yeats-criticism is against me here, but the critics are wrong. *Cuchulain Comforted* does not make full sense unless we understand the precise difference between the supernatural states inhabited in the poem respectively by the Shrouds and by Cuchulain. In terms of Yeats's system, the Shrouds are moving through the last moments of the state called the Shiftings, until in the poem's last line they pass into the state Yeats calls the Beatitude. Cuchulain, less advanced than the Shrouds, moves in the poem from the Phantasmagoria or third phase of the state of Meditation into the Shiftings. To translate this, we need to turn to *A Vision*.

After you die, Yeats tells us there, you find yourself in a state he calls The Vision of the Blood Kindred, a kind of farewell to the sensuous world, to things as they were, to images and impulses. The following state is the Meditation, which is in three phases, called in sequence the Dreaming Back, the Return, and the Phantasmagoria. In the whole of the Meditation your labor is to see your past life as a coherent whole, an achieved form, like a work of art. Yet the Meditation is not a creative state; it is confused, imperfect, unhappy, and begins with the painful Dreaming Back, in which all the events of your past life recur. In the Return phase, which is a kind of antithesis of artistic creation, you deconstruct all the events of your life until they are turned into pure knowledge, divested of all accident, all passion.

You are ready then for the Phantasmagoria, which is where we meet Cuchulain in the poem, leaning upon a tree, suffering again the wounds and blood of his destruction, and so at work exhausting, as Yeats says, "not nature, not pain and pleasure, but emotion." When emotion is exhausted, in this nightmare parody of poetic vision, Cuchulain will be ready to join the Shrouds in the Shiftings, where moral good and moral evil, and particularly courage and cowardice, are cast off by the Spirit. In this shifting of your whole morality as a man, you are emptied out, and are made ready for the Shrouds' tranfiguration into complete equilibrium or wholeness, at once a condition of unconsciousness and an epiphany or privileged moment of consciousness: "They had changed their throats and had the throats of birds."

Though *Cuchulain Comforted* takes you only so far (for dramatic reasons), Yeats's system in *A Vision* takes you all the way back to rebirth again. The Shrouds, and Cuchulain when he is ready, will pass next to the Purification, which means mostly that you become very simple, free of all complexity, in an occult state. You may linger in the Purification for centuries, while your thin Spirit seeks out a living person to somehow help you into the Foreknowledge, a kind of launching pad towards Rebirth.

If we return to *Cuchulain Comforted* with these arbitrary but peculiarly fascinating Yeatsian distinctions firmly in mind, we can begin to understand the poem's design upon us. The cowards, until the last line of the poem, remain cowards, "Mainly because of what we only know/The rattle of those arms makes us afraid." What is it that they know? In the terms of Yeats's system, they know what Cuchulain has not yet realized, that all of us must live again, and since they are not yet in the Beatitude, they retain enough of their nature to fear the hero's weapons. But in deeper terms, belonging to European literary tradition at least since Homer, they know something that humanly impresses us more. They are comforted by their momentary communal experience ("And all we do/All must together do") but they know what Yeats the poet so greatly knows, which is what Homer knew, that in dying as in living any sense of community is rapidly evanescent. Cuchulain may be degraded (if indeed that is Yeats's entire intention, which I doubt), yet he remains the hero. In encountering Cuchulain, who can bear the solitude of dying as he can bear the solitude of being reborn, they encounter their own foreboding that in rebirth they must experience again the condition of being alone, which as cowards they cannot tolerate.

What then is Yeats most crucially saying about death, or rather about dying, in this fascinating but veiled Dantesque poem, with its muted *terza rima*? Very much, I think, what his master Shelley said about death in *Adonais* and *The Triumph of Life* and what his fellow-student of Shelley, Browning, was saying in *Childe Roland to the Dark Tower Came*. The consciousness of death's necessity calls into question the purposiveness of all human action that is not somehow communal, and yet the dignity of dying, for a poet, demands a questing mode of action that is either wholly solitary or that admits the possibility of the community only of a band of brothers, the precursors of poet and hero, or as we now should say, the poet-as-hero. Yeats, as perhaps the last of the High Romantics of European tradition, confirms his tradition's view of death even as he seems to qualify or even degrade it. Death matters because it can be *materia poetica*, but only when it becomes an opportunity for the poet to pass a Last Judgment upon himself. Was he enough of a hero? Did he surmount his precursors, or if he joined them in failure, was he at least worthy of such a joining? Death is, therefore, even for a poet or hero, a social phenomenon essentially, and the standards it must meet (or evade) involve some sort of vision of the communal, however specialized that vision may be.

How un-American this is, and how far even from Emerson, let alone Whitman and Dickinson and their descendants all through American poetry, including Hart Crane and Wallace Stevens. Because our poets are such gorgeous solipsists, from Emerson on, their vision of dying has no relation to this European dialectic of the communal and the solitary. Browning, a passionate egomaniac, is all but selfless compared to Whitman and Dickinson, whose spirits make contact only with divisions in their own selves. Yeats, compared with Wallace Stevens, is drowned in the dramas of other selves; there are *people* in his poems, but Stevens magnificently knows only himself, attaining his greatest peace when he can intone most persuasively:

> And if there is an hour there is a day,
>
> There is a month, a year, there is a time
> In which majesty is a mirror of the self:
> I have not but I am and as I am, I am.

What can so great an "I am" meditate when it comes into the region where we all must die? Browning is not a better poet than Dickinson, or Yeats than Stevens; the problem here is not one of aesthetic loss and gain, but of an imaginative difference that I am rather dismayed to find may be at its root a social difference. Our native strain goes down deeper still, and must be related to the differences between British and American Puritanism, since both poetries for the last two hundred years are, in a clear sense, displaced Protestantisms. But rather than lose myself in a labyrinth I am not competent to explore, I want to return us to a text, with a brief overview of Stevens' *The Owl in the Sarcophagus,* after which I will conclude with a contrast between Yeats and Stevens as representative British and American poets of death.

The Owl in the Sarcophagus is an elegy for Stevens' friend, Henry Church, to whom *Notes toward a Supreme Fiction* had been dedicated. Written in 1947, when Stevens was sixty-eight, it is also a kind of pre-elegy for Stevens' own death, some eight years later. In Stevens' work, it stands chronologically and thematically between *Credences of Summer,* essentially a celebratory, naturalistic, Keatsian poem, and *The Auroras of Autumn,* a Wordsworthian poem of natural loss, and of the compensatory imagination rising up, not to redress loss, but to intimate what Stevens beautifully calls "an innocence of the earth." *The Owl in*

the Sarcophagus yields up the world celebrated, however quali-
fiedly, in *Credences of Summer* and reaches towards the divination
of *The Auroras of Autumn,* where the only consolation offered is
the wisdom of acceptance, of completion, a wisdom testifying to the
mind's power over our consciousness of death. *The Owl in the
Sarcophagus* does not go so far; it does not leave us with Stevens'
"The vital, the never-failing genius,/Fulfilling his meditations,
great and small." But it does give us a lasting sense of "the beings
of the mind/In the light-bound space of the mind, the floreate
flare . . ." or more starkly of what Stevens also calls "the mythology
of modern death."

The Owl in the Sarcophagus is a vision of two forms that move
among the dead, "high sleep" and "high peace," two brothers,
and a third form, "the mother of us all,/The earthly mother and
the mother of/The dead." This is an American Orphic Trinity,
ultimately derived from Emerson, though Stevens was evidently
not wholly aware of his full relation to this particular precursor.
Stevens' "high sleep" is a version of Dionysus, however strange or
even oxymoronic the image of a Dionysiac sleep must seem. But
then, Stevens' "high peace" is a transformed Eros, and an erotic
peace is rather far from the experience of most of us. The Orphic
Great Mother, probably derived by Stevens from Whitman's *The
Sleepers,* is a transfigured Ananke, Necessity divested of her dread
and made into a figure of ultimate consolation (as she is also in
certain passages of Emerson's *The Conduct of Life*). In Stevens'
elegy, the consolation is attained by a magical metamorphosis of
the mind's consciousness of death into the opposite of such consciousness, a child asleep in its own life:

> These are death's own supremest images,
> The pure perfections of parental space,
>
> The children of a desire that is the will,
> Even of death, the beings of the mind
> In the light-bound space of the mind, the floreate flare

It is a child that sings itself to sleep,
The mind, among the creatures that it makes,
The people, those by which it lives and dies.

When we contrast Stevens and Yeats on death, we might begin
by remembering Stevens' insistence that poetry must satisfy the
human desire for resemblances. Against *A Vision*'s multi-phased
life-after-death or rather death-between-lives, we can set a sardonic
prose statement by Stevens:

> What a ghastly situation it would be if the world of the dead
> was actually different from the world of the living and, if as life
> ends, instead of passing to a former Victorian sphere, we passed
> into a land in which none of our problems had been solved, after
> all, and nothing resembled anything else in shape, in color, in
> sound, in look or otherwise.

The world of the dead in *The Owl in the Sarcophagus* is only
what, "Generations of the imagination piled/In the manner of its
stitchings," and Stevens speaks of his mother of the dead as "losing
in self/The sense of self," very much in Dickinson's manner. His
elegy is profoundly American in making dying an ultimate
solipsistic adventure, at once Bacchic, erotic and necessitarian, and
as much an act of solitary fulfillment as the writing of a poem is.
Dying has priority in divination, even as becoming a poet estab-
lishes priority in divination. Major American poets see dying
as only another assertion in the self's expansiveness, another huge
effort to subsume the universe. Dying, whatever else it is for our
native strain, for the genius of America, is not a social act. Even
Yeats knows what European poets always knew, that dying makes a
gesture towards community, but the American imagination has
another goal always.

The greatness of *Cuchulain Comforted* is that, like *The Man
and the Echo* and certain other late poems of Yeats, it shows its
poet both powerfully employing and yet standing clear of his
own mythologies. This is his advantage over Stevens, and the

general advantage of the less solipsistic British over our own poets. Still, the whole movement of modern poetry is towards a progressive internalization of every sort of quest, and Yeats is most Romantic and most like American poets when he defies everything that is external and societal. Against *Cuchulain Comforted,* with all its magnificence of Yeats-against-Yeats, its seeming degradation of heroism, we can set Yeats himself, in a late prose manifesto, celebrating the unique power of the poets: "The world knows nothing because it has made nothing, we know everything because we have made everything."

THE SACRAL POWER OF DEATH IN CONTEMPORARY EXPERIENCE

BY WILLIAM F. MAY

Is there any justification for talking about the sacral power of death in contemporary experience? From one perspective it would appear that modern culture has become increasingly secular—and secular without significant remainder. Modern man has freed himself from the incubus of religion; he is pressing forward into the full measure of his manhood and maturity; his style, autonomous; his landscape, this-worldly and profane; and his hopes for the future, largely invested in the accomplishments of science and technology.

This essay is written in the conviction that the assumption of secularity is diagnostically false. Modern culture reeks of religion and those who want contact with the modern world will need to acknowledge this fact. Our attitudes toward death are a case in point. But to argue the point it will be necessary, in the first part of this essay, to develop religious categories appropriate to the contemporary experience of death. Only then will it be possible to proceed to the philosophical interpretation of this religious reality and finally to the practical import of both analyses for the behavior of the "helping professions" toward the dying.

I. RELIGIOUS CATEGORIES AND THE CONTEMPORARY RESPONSE TO DEATH

We may, of course, be justifiably hesitant about applying religious categories to the current experience of death if the word "religion" is exclusively associated with the official religious tradition of Christianity that has functioned as the source of unity for western civilization. Religion, so understood, is the glue that holds a civilization together. The belief in God (and the practices associated with that belief) has regulated the public life of western man—his social, economic, and political institutions, and interpreted and directed his private life—the ordering of his sexuality, his family life, his leisure, and his death.

Clearly, today, the regulatory power of the official religious tradition of the West has diminished; Constantinian Christianity no longer dominates the age. Whatever comprehensive ordering of experience and behavior we know, including the experience of death, does not conform to the traditional patterns of Judaism and Christianity. This is why the popular diagnosticians of our time, from the Comtean positivists forward, have argued that the modern world is increasingly secular.

But religious phenomena cannot be restricted exclusively to those official religious traditions that hold a civilization together; they must also include variant experiences of sacred power and patterns of religious behavior that may beset a culture in convulsive change and turmoil. Such religious forces may be quite unofficial, non-traditional, even anti-traditional, yet they are potent in human affairs. Indeed, they may add to the strains and crises which the civilization experiences both in the political domain and in the arena of personal behavior.

The need to broaden the term "religion" would be fairly obvious if we were to delineate in this essay religious patterns at work in contemporary politics. Some of the most powerful movements in American political life across the past twenty years have reflected religious patterns; but all, in their differing ways, have been opposed to institutional Christianity.[1] Similarly, the re-

---

[1] The Radical Right has been given to a kind of Manichaean dualism in politics, identifying the kingdom of God with Capitalist America and the kingdom of Satan with the Communist East. So far removed is this religious view from traditional Christianity that fanatics on the Right have suspected all established institutions, the church included, as the instruments of their satanic foe. Conservatism, meanwhile, has conformed to the Babylonian creation myth in its politics: Marduk vs. Tiamat, law and order vs. chaos, Ronald Reagan vs. Berkeley. Given his abhorrence of chaos, the conservative has been outraged by a prophetic Christianity that runs the risk of producing turmoil through its social criticism. The New Left, finally, has

ligious element in the modern experience of death does not conform to traditional Christianity and its variously stated doctrines of the immortality of the soul or the resurrection of the body. In fact, modern religious apprehensions about death are such as to undermine these traditional Christian teachings. The term "religious" needs to be broadened. We need a definition that will push behind all the familiar associations of the word with the developed denominations and theologies of the West.

According to the phenomenologists of religion, who can help with the meaning of the term, religion does not have a primary reference to deity. The "gods," argues Van der Leeuw, were a relative latecomer on the scene. At its root, religion consists of some kind of experience of sacred power. This power may appear in many ways. For Israel, sacred power meant the God who made a startling show of his strength on behalf of the Israelites in a contest with the power of the Pharoah and who bound them over to Himself forever at Mt. Sinai. For others, the sacred may appear as fate, a power that gives and takes away, lifts up and casts down in a fashion so voiceless and unhearing that it cannot even be called cruel. Fatalism was powerful in urban culture at the decline of the Roman Empire and we hear faint echoes of it again on the lips of sweet innocents—"that's the way the ball bounces," "that's the way the cookie crumbles."

However it shows itself, the sacred is distinguished from ordinary profane power in that it does not appear as something that man can fully master and use toward his own appointed ends. It confounds the efforts of the practical man to control it and the contemplative man to know it. It is full of surprises and therefore it insists upon its own unfolding, refusing to submit to

reflected both an inverse Manichaeism amongst the militants and a mystic yearning for immediacy amongst the pacifists and others, as they withdraw from the prosaic and oppressive patterns of institutional life, Christianity included. All of these movements have been virulently religious and equally dissatisfied with institutional Christianity. For an expansion of the author's argument on these matters, see "Manichaeism in American Politics," *Christianity and Crisis*, Vol. XXVI, No. 7 (May 2, 1966), pp. 85–89, and "The Mythic Foundations of the Politics of the Conservative," *Soundings*, Vol. 53, No. 1 (Spring 1970), pp. 20–45.

the normal procedures by which ordinary, profane, secular man handles his life.

Long before there were official gods, religion meant most simply "alertness" or "attentiveness." The sacred always approaches as the overpowering. When it appears, there can be no attending to something else. That is why at the level of cultic routine we use the phrase, "religious observance." The religious man is watchful, wakeful, and observant before a highly charged potency. There is nothing to be done toward the sacred except to let it be what it is, permit it to run its course, and let one's own life be caught up in its force. Gripped by its power, a man's attitude is highly ambivalent: he neither moves easily toward the sacred nor casually away from it. He experiences longing tempered by fear, and fear given to shy approach.

This is the attitude toward death that one finds in literature at the turn of the twentieth century, especially in literature sited in the city. The century opens with the prophetic *Dubliners* of James Joyce, in the first chapter of which a young boy—friend to a dying priest—muses on the word "paralysis" and offers therein a fine description of religious awe.

> " 'Paralysis'—it sounded to me like the name of a maleficent and sinful being. It filled me with fear and yet I longed to be near it and to look upon its deadly work."

Joyce captures beautifully that ambivalence of spirit that the phenomenologists have recognized in all religious feeling and which they have variously termed: "awe," "dread," "astonishment," "wonder," or "amazement." A peculiar ambivalence, a strange vibration, a sort of motionless motion obtains in the religious man, an attentiveness somewhat akin to the attention that a hummingbird gives to a flower, when its wings beat furiously and yet it hovers at the spot. This, apparently, is the way men relate to death when they open themselves to its dreadful reality.

The "object" of this feeling, of course, is hardly the traditional God of Christians and Jews. Destructive power and death, not life, is the object of awe. In *Ulysses*, Joyce used a particularly gloomy expression to convey this sense of the supremacy of destructive power—"Dio Boia"—the "hangman God." So understood, death is not interpreted merely as the biological incident that ends human life. It appears in all those destructive forces in the course of life that grip the heart with love, fear, hope, worry, and flight, long before the end is reached. Whenever the concert is over, the meal is digested, or the career turns barren in one's hands, a man experiences the quiet, disturbing fall from life to death.

It is difficult to do justice to the perceived scope of destructive power without falling into parody of the Psalmist's sense of the omnipresence of God. The power that brings death besets men on every side. It drives men from behind as they flee into frenetic activities—the pursuit of career, virtuosity, or the display of some glory—hoping to escape their metaphysical solitude by outlining themselves against a dark background. It confronts men frontally as they mount their battles against their threatening enemies, whether that enemy happens to be soldier, competitor, or sibling. It lies in wait and ambushes from the side—the young, the high-minded, the hedonist, and the frivolous—with the unexpectedness of a clipping at a football game. It stirs beneath human life in the profoundest of pleasures, as it touches with melancholy the marriage bed or as it ladens with guilt the relations between the generations. And at night, it settles down from above and breathes gently within old men who are weary with all other forms of fleeing, fighting, and sidestepping death and who long now for sleep and the surcease of care.

Yet, after this pessimistic streak in our literature has been given its due, does it not exaggerate? The dominant cultural fact of our time is the emergence of technology which has made possible the spectacular enlargement, differentiation, and sophistication of human powers to cope with threats from the environment.

Let the novelists and poets continue to reify, deify, or demonize death; more significant in the long run is the increasing subjection of the process of dying and death to rational, technical, specialized control. From this second perspective, the contemporary attitude toward death appears to be increasingly secular rather than religious. The objective ground for this triumph over death is the whole development of the modern apparatus of medical care, from preventive medicine, through the specialized staffs of the modern hospital and nursing home, elaborately differentiated to cope with acute and chronic illness, including the near-omniscient monitoring of the intensive care units, and concluding more recently with the ingenious salvaging of organs from the corpse. Nothing, argues one historian of science, has more affected the quality of life in the last two hundred years and our objective capacity to cope with the powers that beset us than the application of technology to disease and death.

Recently, however, it has become less clear that these technological feats have been accompanied by a corresponding inner confidence in our relationships to death. We arrange for the marvels of modern medical care, because, to be sure, we desire the recovery of the sick but also because these devices offer us a means of avoiding sickness, aging, and dying. In the language of the sociologists, the *manifest* function of our cadre of experts in the helping professions is to provide the critically ill with better cure and care, but a *latent* social function of this specialization is the avoidance of an event with which we cannot cope. If, moreover, the studies of doctors' attitudes toward dying can be credited (which indicate that doctors as a professional class are more prone than others to the fear of death), it would seem that we have surrendered the dying with near-perfect precision into the hands of those who will maintain those patterns of evasion which led us originally to remove the dying from sight.

Seen in this light, the subsequent resort to technology in preparing the corpse for burial is all of a piece with the preceding career of the dying man. This is the material already covered by the British satirists (Aldous Huxley, *After Many a Summer;* Evelyn Waugh, *The Loved One;* Muriel Spark, *Memento Mori;* and more recently, Jessica Mitford, *The American Way of Death*). Uncle John cannot be allowed to die and repose in solemn dignity. He must be prettied up with rouge and cheap satin, his face molded into a smile. It is not simply his beautification but his beatification that the mortician attempts to achieve. Poor Uncle John never smiled in his life, but now he does—beatifically. The church won't canonize him, but the mortician will. We are supposed to look on the very face of the corpse and say about Uncle John, "Doesn't he look natural?"—which, of course, is the one thing he doesn't look.

The satirists are wrong, however, insofar as they impute to Americans a belief in the triumph of technology over death. Our strategies and rites are evasive not because Americans react to death as trivial or incidental, but because they feel an inner sense of bankruptcy before it. The attempts at evasion and concealment are pathetic rather than casual. The doctor's substitute diagnoses and vague replies, and the undertaker's allusions to "the beautiful memory picture" reflect a culture in which men sense their own poverty before the event.

Men evade death because they recognize in the event an immensity that towers above their resources for handling it. In effect, death (or the reality that brings it) is recognized as a sacred power that confounds the efforts of men to master it. A heavy silence surrounds death. This painful reticence has a source more profound than our childlike submission to the advice of a doctor. Silence has its origin in the awesomeness of death itself. Just as the Jew, out of respect for the awesomeness of God, would not pronounce the name of Jahweh, so we find it difficult to bring the word death to our lips in the presence of its power. This is so because we are at a loss as to how to proceed on the far side of this word. Our philosophies and our moralities desert us. They retreat and leave us wordless. Their rhetoric, which seemed so suitable on other occasions, suddenly loses it power, and we may well wonder whether our words them-selves are not caught up in a massive, verbose, uneasy flight from death, while we are left with nothing to say, except to "say it with flowers."

The underlying pessimism of these patterns of avoidance is consistent with the preoccupation with death that was identified earlier in the works of James Joyce. In both cases, death is reckoned with as destructive power. This pessimistic streak, moreover, is not confined to our so-called serious literature. Death and violence are an obsessive theme in our popular culture as well. The headlines in our daily newspapers are almost exclusively devoted to telling us what death has accomplished in the last twenty-four hours. The first three pages of an issue of the Chicago *Sun-Times,* chosen at random, carried the fol-lowing headlines:

51 Escape Death in Fiery Jetliner Crash, 2 Killed

Six Basques Condemned to Die

3 Get Double Death Sentences

Smog Briefly Reaches Danger Level Here

Trio Seized at Farm in Canada Slaying

By Hovering in a Helicopter over Chicago and 3 Other Cities Scientists Have Been Able to Detect Relatively High Levels of Mercury Coming out of the Smokestacks.

Only death—not life—has sufficient energy, vitality, and lure to command the morning headlines and to reduce men to attentive-ness before it, like a priest at his daily devotions.

The analysis so far has indicated two basic responses to the event of death in contemporary culture: on the one hand, the avoidance of death; on the other hand, a preoccupation with death as a destructive and catastrophic event. The category of the sacred explains their connection. Men are tempted simul-taneously to conceal death and to hold themselves enthralled before it, because they recognize death as an overmastering power before which other responses seem unavailing.

In his essay, "The Pornography of Death," Geoffrey Gorer, the English social anthropologist, brings together the phenomena of obsession and concealment by appeal to the religious category of *tabu*. The ambivalence of contemporary responses to death compares structurally to the ambivalence of Victorian attitudes toward sex. A prudish culture in which sexual life was a *tabu* subject developed simultaneously a pornographic obsession with sex. (Gorer defines sexual pornography as an obsession with the sex act abstracted from its natural human emotion, which is affection.) Contemporary culture has substituted death for sex as its *tabu,* its unmentionable event. Correspondingly, contemporary people have been given to a pornographic obsession with death and violence. (In this case, however, pornography means obsession with death abstracted from its natural human emotion, which is grief.)

It should be observed that not all social scientists agree with Gorer. Most notably, Talcott Parsons and Victor Lidz, in their article, "Death in American Society," [2] criticize the commonly held assumption that ". . . the realities of death are characteristically met with 'denial' in contemporary American society. . . ." [3] The position adopted in that paper counters so completely the line of interpretation taken so far in this essay that their thesis deserves treatment and initial response before proceeding any further.

Parsons and Lidz argue that Americans respond to death in a manner consistent with their general orientation to life, which may be summarized as "instrumental activism." Since an important component of this instrumental activism is the scientific method, and since scientists are committed to realism, one should not expect to find "an attitude so drastically discrepant with the realism of science in an area so close to biology and medicine." [4]

[2] In *Essays In Self-Destruction*, Edwin S. Shneidman, ed., New York (Science House, Inc., 1967), Ch. 7.

[3] *Ibid.*, p. 133.

[4] *Ibid.*, p. 134.

Consistent with its instrumental activism, our society distinguishes between death as the natural and inevitable (and desirable) term of human life, which it strives in its ceremonies to accept, and adventitious, premature death which it has increasingly subjected to prevention and/or control. Medicine has made spectacular strides in eliminating or reducing adventitious death (and the suffering that attends dying); people can increasingly look forward to living out their term. Meanwhile, the funeral industry has developed ceremonies of acceptance not too inconsistent with the symbolic needs of a society given to our basic orientation. Funeral caskets, embalming techniques, cosmetic preparations and the showcase layout of the corpse are not elements in a total strategy of denial; each has its reasonable place in a society given to instrumental activism and naturalism about dying. Thus, funeral caskets and embalming techniques were sensible developments for allowing distant relatives and friends to gather under the conditions of a highly mobile society. Cosmetic preparations and certain symbolic reminders of vocation and achievement in the layout of the corpse help to remind the bereaved of the deceased's own role in an instrumental activist society. Further, the customs of the parlor fittingly conspire to reduce the suffering of the bereaved, just as the technology of medicine sought to control the suffering of the deceased in the earlier course of his dying. Only those given to morbidity would equate realism with dwelling on the harsher aspects of death and charge current practice with denial.

A potential terminological confusion should be removed at the outset in a reply to this line of interpretation. Along with Parsons and Lidz, I would agree that Americans do not blindly deny death. The more accurate term is "avoidance" rather than "denial." The man who elaborates ways to avoid what he cannot cope with does not deny it; with every twist and turn of his life, he confesses to its reality for him. This preliminary observation, of course, does not bring this essay any closer to the

Parsons and Lidz position because they would dispute with equal force the validity of the term, "avoidance."

The key issues are whether inevitable death and adventitious death are really subject to the kind of realistic and calm social acceptance and control to which the authors refer. First, it would be easier to interpret current American funeral practice as an expression of a calm acceptance of the natural term of life, if these rites were, in fact, preceded by a mode of truth-telling in the relations of doctor, patient, family, and friends. It is a notable omission in their article, however, that it *assumes* the realism of science and medicine but neglects altogether a sociological investigation or a review of the literature on the actual patterns of behavior toward the dying amongst medical professionals. If, in the course of the career of the dying man, we have not related to his death as a natural event, it is hard to credit a funeral layout which pretends that we have so faced it all along.

Second, the successes of medical technology in the reduction of physical suffering and in the control of adventitious death have not generated subjectively a corresponding optimism about death. Such optimism alone would allow us to find somewhat more socially coherent the current rituals of the funeral parlor. The front page of the newspaper does not give a picture of adventitious death retreating before the triumphal march of technology. Quite the contrary, the initiative in the newspapers belongs to death and destructive power. The initiative is also there in the dream-life of men, in the apprehensions of children, in the compulsions of the overworked, in the isolation of the hospital ward, and in the anxieties of a sleepless night. If the social system were more profoundly positive in its response to death, one would not expect to find the psyche so easily jangled by the threat of impending catastrophe.

These criticisms are quite limited in that they operate within the basic tests for reality that Parsons and Lidz as sociologists presuppose. How does one, after all, "prove" that something exists in experience that is being avoided? A major test for Parsons and Lidz seems to be that the American mode of response to death is "appropriate to our primary cultural patterns of activism." [5] The primary test is whether the response coheres with the American social system. Leaving aside the question of all other manner of tests—philosophical, theological, literary or psychological—I do not find the systematic response to death and dying as smoothly functional and reinforcing as the essay suggests. In this, perhaps, there is a clue that the symbol system of the society fails to correspond to the exigencies of the human reality.

This diagnostic section of the paper should not be closed, however, without acknowledging that quite recently in American life certain changes have occurred that open up the possibility of movement beyond the twin responses of concealment and obsession. Measured against the total organization of the culture, these changes in attitude toward death may seem quite modest, but they should not go unnoticed. A literature has begun to develop on the subjects of both concealment and obsession. Clearly our personal and institutional avoidance of responsibility toward the aged and the dying has received recently a great deal of public and professional attention, and our preoccupations with death and violence have been subject to considerable analysis.

Once a society develops a certain measure of self-consciousness about a problem, the problem is no longer quite the same. The age of conformity generated so much literature about conformity that the culture to a certain degree was thrown outside the phenomenon described. This measure of transcendence through awareness does not in itself dissolve a problem, but it does open up the possibility of moving beyond certain institutional reflexes and responses. Diagnosis itself generates the possibility of certain prescriptive moves which in this case will await discussion in the third section of this paper.

[5] *Ibid.*, p. 134.

II. PHILOSOPHICAL REFLECTION ON FLIGHT AND PREOCCUPATION WITH DEATH

The major philosophical statement about the two responses outlined so far in this paper is found in the work of Martin Heidegger, the German existentialist. For Heidegger, a man's authentic existence is a being-toward-death; his inauthentic existence, a flight from his end. Man may either open himself up in anxiety before death or attempt to determine his life in such a way as to evade and conceal his end. Clearly, in his major work, *Being and Time,* these responses are not offered indifferently as symmetrical alternatives. Despite his own quest for neutral language, Heidegger invests the alternative of being-toward-death with a priority that is religious in its proportions.

Man flees from his death into the shelter of the anonymous collective, into the apparent solidities of his work-life, or into the deliverances of objective thought. From Heidegger's point of view, the evasion of death in any of these forms is simultaneously self-evasion; for only in anxiety before death does man come to himself. Only in the project toward his end does a man recover himself from a life of self-abandonment and flight. A man's relationship to death therefore is not merely one in a series of possible relations which are authentic or inauthentic, standing alongside his relationship to wife, job, or creativity. An authentic relationship to death is the touchstone of authenticity toward all else. Man is essentially himself only in his being-toward-death. In projecting toward death, a man is individualized. He is drawn out of the life of the anonymous collective and offered his own induplicable name.

Without seeking to reduce Heidegger's sense of death to its historical context alone, we may note its appropriateness to a culture whose chief problem is that it absorbs its members into a massive, anonymous, impersonal life. In this context, death appears as the great individualizer. As the folk song puts it (mercifully free of Heideggerian jargon):

You've got to cross that lonesome valley,
You've got to cross it by yourself.
Cain't no one cross it for you,
You've got to cross it by yourself.

A fascinating cross-cultural study can be made between the contemporary and the late medieval sense of death. Without reducing the medieval sense of death to its cultural context alone, we may note that death appears there not so much as the individualizer but as the leveler of men. This symbolization is correspondingly appropriate to the problem of a hierarchical society. A people who had endured the distinctions and abuses inflicted upon men by the privileges of birth might well appreciate the high vengeance of their overthrowal by death. Thus at the Cemetery of the Innocents in Paris the bones of dukes and serfs, bishops and charwomen were heaped together in the same charnel house. Death brought the common and the uncommon to a common end. Moreover, the *Danse Macabre* of the period, in fresco and wood-engraving, reflected the same theme. The jaunty figures and symbols of death in the dance of death could afford to be overfamiliar with their living partners—tugging at fine clothes, taunting the highborn—because they would soon disrobe them. The doctor would be robbed of his healing power, the woman of her beauty, the bourgeois of his money, and the soldier of his authority.[6] Death could be outrageously impudent, ignoring the proprieties that ordinarily obtain between men in a hierarchical society, because it would soon possess the living by dispossessing them. The death dance "preached social equality as the Middle Ages understood it, Death leveling the various ranks and professions."[7]

Whether viewed as individualizer or leveler, death in these cases functions as social critic. We normally think of the trauma

[6] Émile Mâle, *Religious Art from the Twelfth to the Eighteenth Century*, New York (The Noonday Press, 1958), pp. 142–155.
[7] Huizinga, *The Waning of the Middle Ages*, New York (Doubleday & Company, Inc., 1954), p. 146.

of dying as exposing a man in the literal sense of the word, in that it places him out in the open, outside the shelter of his environment and culture.   At the same time, however, it exposes his culture to view.   It allows him to see his culture as a stranger, in the oppressiveness and hypocrisy of its social forms, whether the oppressiveness of a hierarchical society or the gray conformities of a mass society.   The sociologists have thus associated the trauma of death with the experience of social *anomie*.   (The most impressive statement of this point is found not in theological, sociological, or philosophical literature, but in that stunning critique of professional and middle class Russian society compacted within forty pages by Tolstoi in *The Death of Ivan Ilych*.)

The usual criticism of Heidegger is that he is excessively gloomy, negative, and nihilistic, locating a project toward death at the very heart of human existence.   He represents a tortuous German romanticism in philosophy whose passing the Anglo-Saxon world is not likely to mourn.   Some moralists have even argued that existentialist talk about anxiety before death has itself contributed to the fear of death in our time.

This charge of morbidity does not seem to me to be the most fundamental objection to Heidegger's position, and this for several reasons.   First, any comparative study of morbidity must concede the existence of two breeds of gloomy men: those who think about death all the time and those who never think about it.   An apparently life-centered culture that systematically relegates the dying to indignity, humiliation, and oblivion because it cannot stand to be reminded of its own poverty of resources before death is vastly more morbid on the subject than the philosopher who reckons with dying as a human possibility. Heidegger, whether rightly or not, humanizes death.   "It is no longer death, but I who am dying," says one of the heroes in a novel by Malraux *(The Royal Way)*.

This kind of romantic talk is not at all a cringing, terror-stricken response to death but actually speech in an heroic mold. Heidegger, in fact, is very explicit about this when he distinguishes carefully between the responses of fear and anxiety, only the latter of which properly characterizes an authentic response to death. Fear is distinguished from anxiety in that it always has an object. In fear, man cringes before the menacing—all those things that threaten him and his loves. Anxiety, however, is that peculiar feeling that has no object; it is rather a dread of nothing—nothing in particular. When man is anxious in this special sense toward death, he is in dread not of something destructive that menaces him, but rather of nothing. When man so responds to death, he is finally confronted only with his own freedom—the nothingness of his own freedom—his freedom as pure possibility which he holds in his own hands and resolve. Thus anxiety before death is quickly transfigured into self-confrontation. The ordinary kind of dread before death as destructive power, with which our paper began in the first section, has been dissolved. Anxiety before death has become freedom's own emotional reflex upon itself.

A second line of criticism of Heidegger's philosophy of death would take therefore quite the opposite tack—not that he exaggerates death but that he fails to reckon with the concrete threat of death as men experience it. Accordingly, Arland Ussher, the Irish critic, wrote,

> Dr. Heidegger sits among the immortals—like one of the fabled Himalayan sages, waiting for new Gods to be born out of the pool of Nothingness. He seems to have lost sight of one small matter— one thing which he of all men should have remembered—a thing by which more sensitive, if less subtle, minds have been more than usually troubled in the 1940's. He has forgotten to all appearance that men must die.[8]

Dr. Joseph Rheingold of the Harvard Medical School has sought to give psychological filling to this judgment against Heidegger in his book, *The Mother, Anxiety, and Death,* in which he argues that "Being is not threatened and penetrated by non-being, as Heidegger believes, but by danger of catastrophic

[8] Arland Ussher, *Journey Through Dread,* New York (The Devin-Adair Company, 1955), p. 92.

death." [9]   Rheingold asserts that man's basic anxiety is directed to catastrophic death or what I have termed destructive power. As might be anticipated in this psychoanalytic account, the child exposes the real experience of death. The child does not reduce death to a natural experience, as recorded in the proposition that all creatures die. Rather he feels keenly the danger of being mutilated, killed, dismembered, suffocated, immobilized, deprived of sight, and abandoned. All later threats of death reinstate the infant's terror, a terror which is focussed originally on his fear of injury and abandonment at the hands of the mother. Rheingold's position, of course, helps explain psychologically why men believe that death is not merely impersonal fact but malign fate at the hands of a powerful agency.

Rheingold's pervasive gloom about the human condition need not be accepted in order to criticize Heidegger. But the prior fault for Heidegger's failure to appreciate fully the threat of death lies in his anthropology. Unfortunately, he depresses the significance of man's identity with his flesh and community, those identities which the event of death threatens with catastrophe.

This paper will close therefore with an attempt to offer a constructive analysis of man's identities with both his flesh and his community, analysis of a kind lacking in Heidegger but needed to interpret both the crisis of death and our human resources for responding to the event. Certain implications will be drawn from this anthropological statement for the work of the helping professions.

III. The Twofold Crisis of Death and the Care of the Dying

A. The Crisis of the Flesh

Heidegger ignores the somatic dimensions of death. Quite legitimately, he criticizes those who reduce death to a biological

---

[9] Joseph C. Rheingold, *The Mother, Anxiety, and Death: The Catastrophic Death Complex*, Boston (Little, Brown & Co., 1967), p. 228.

incident alone, but he makes the opposite mistake of ignoring the significance for man of the biological crisis of dying: specifically, he ignores the suffering of the body, and the moral and spiritual problems it creates.

A man is identified with his flesh. He is not a ghost. The body is more important to his identity than words to a poet. Part of the terror of death is that it threatens a man with a loss of identity with his flesh, an identity which is essential to him in at least three ways.

First, man's flesh is the means to his *control* of his world. Except as he uses his flesh instrumentally (feet for walking, hands for working, tongue for talking), he could not relate to the world by way of mastery and control. When death therefore threatens to separate him from his flesh, it threatens him first with a comprehensive loss of possession and control of his universe. Death meets him as the dispossessor—even though man retaliates as best he can with an assortment of insurance policies. Quite shrewdly, the medieval moralists saw a special connection between the capital sin of avarice and old age. Avarice is the special sin in which a man focusses his life on his possessions. The closer a man gets to the time of his dispossession, the more fiercely he clings to what he has and the more suspicion he feels toward all those who would dispossess him with indecorous haste.

Suppose that a man who has brutally exploited his body as an instrument of aggression against his world suddenly suffers a heart attack. The very flesh through which he exerted mastery explodes from within. He is helpless in the hands of others, unable even to control noises down the hall that disturb his sleep. Under these circumstances, the apparatus of medicine, even while ministering to him, reminds him of his helplessness and therefore of the poverty of all his attempts to solve the problem of his existence through mastery alone.

The situation is catastrophic in the literal sense of a sudden reversal—the person who is accustomed to adult mastery is suddenly reduced to the circumstance of a relatively helpless child.

Hence the inevitable response of the dying to their plight which Dr. Kubler-Ross has identified as anger and desperate bargaining —both responses to the catastrophe of loss of control.

The implications for the helping professions in this situation are clear. The patient mut be allowed to participate in decisions as much as possible. If, however, he is systematically deprived of accurate knowledge about his condition, he has already been deprived of the decision-making power of a rational man. He is wholly directed from the outside—a deprivation already institutionalized in the phrase, the *management* of the terminal patient.

Second, a man's flesh is more than his means to world-mastery, it is also the site for the disclosure of the world to him in its uncontrolled splendor and diversity. Except as flesh is sensitive, susceptible, and vulnerable, a man could not be open to the world as it pours in upon him in a wild profusion of colors, sounds, and feelings. When death therefore threatens to separate him from his flesh, it threatens also to separate him from the propertyless creation which is his for the beholding and savoring in ritual, art, and daily routine. This process of separation already begins with the removal of the aged to the relatively impoverished, salt-free environment of the old people's home. It continues when the apparatus of medicine, dedicated as it is to the recovery of mastery, presents the patient with a functional but blank environment, devoid of the irrelevant details that make up a truly human existence. Yeats once complained about the abstraction of the formula, H_2O, by observing, "I like a little seaweed in my definition of water."

The implications for the social network of care are clear. Some European societies provide home visitation services, including a daily hot meal for the aged, that permit them to remain in an environment where memory and savoring still function. Some European hospitals manage to maintain gardens as part of their grounds. A garden is a functionally irrelevant expense, perhaps, in an institution dedicated to treating and discharging people as fast as it can; but some patients, after all, are discharged only for burial and it is well to maintain for them a sign of a world that has not shrunk to the final abstraction of their irremedial pain.

Third, the flesh is more than instrumental to control and more than sensitive, it is also revelatory. A man reveals himself to his neighbor in and through the living flesh. He is one with his countenance, gestures, and the physical details of his speech. As some have put it, he not only *has* a body, he *is* his body. Part of the terror of death, then, is that it threatens him with a loss of his revelatory power. The dreadfulness of the corpse lies in its claim to be the body of the person, while it is wholly unrevealing of the person. What was once so expressive of the human soul has suddenly become a mask.

At the very least, this third crisis for the flesh is warrant for a greater social investment in the services of care, as opposed to a rather exclusive orientation to cure. If the restoration of individuals to mastery were the only issue, then we might be morally free to make a cold calculus as to social worth and count only cure important. If, however, a man *is* his body, then caring should extend to the humblest of details of eating and cleansing, especially during that difficult time when infirmities humiliate, when they keep the body from expressing the soul in its full dignity. Upon death, moreover, there is warrant for a funeral service in which the body is not treated as a disposable cartridge to be thrown away like garbage. Such argument, however, for a fitting disposal of the remains, whether by cremation or burial, is hardly an apology for present-day funeral practices. Quite the contrary, it opens the way for an even more savage criticism of those practices in which the body becomes the lewd object of the mortician's craft. It is one thing to minimize the violence done to the body by death. It is quite another thing to impose upon the corpse the appearance of a character other than its own. Let death be death. There is no reason to add to its hideousness by mocking the inability of the dead to reveal themselves.

B. The Crisis of Community

Death means separation not only from flesh but from community as well. This threat has already been anticipated in the discussion of the revelatory power of the flesh. Death unravels human community, dividing husband and wife, father and son, and lovers from one another. Not even the child is exempt from this threat. In demanding the reassurance of a voice, the touch of a hand at bedtime, he shows that he knows all the essential issues involved in a sleep that is early practice in dying. Death threatens all men with final abandonment, exclusion, and oblivion.

Again, this threat is operative beforehand in the crisis of dying and the response of the community to this crisis. One of the most devastating features of terminal illness is the fear of abandonment. Sickness has already isolated the patient from his normal identity in the community; strong and authoritative, he is now relatively helpless; gregarious by nature, he suddenly finds friends exhausting. Ironically, the very apparatus by which the community ministers to his physical need isolates him further. The modern hospital segregates the sick and the dying from their normal human resources. As doctors have observed, in an Arabian village, a grandmother dies in the midst of her children and grandchildren, cows and donkeys. But our high level of technological development leads simply to dying a death appropriate to one's disease—in the heart ward or the cancer ward.[10]

Most desolating of all is the breakdown of communication between the dying patient, the doctor, and the nearest of kin. Substitute diagnoses are sometimes justified on the grounds that they establish an emotional equilibrium (homeostasis) essential to the health and comfort of the patient, but the spiritual effect of

[10] See comments by Drs. Bryant M. Wedge and Robert H. Dovenmuchle in "Death and Dying: Attitudes of Patient and Doctor," Symposium No. 11, *Group For the Advancement of Psychiatry*, New York (Mental Health Materials Center, 1965), pp. 648, 652.

evasiveness can itself be emotionally disturbing. It is demoralizing for everybody concerned to get stuck with a lie, because, once told, life tends to organize itself around it. Even when the lie is not working, even when it produces the anguish of suspicion, isolation, resentment, and uncertainty, the doctor and family may rely on it to keep *their own* relations to the patient in a state of equilibrium. It seems too late for everybody concerned to recover an authentic relationship to the event. Isolated by evasion and lies, the patient is driven out of community before his time. He has forced upon him a premature burial. While trying to avoid the fact of death, the community actually reeks of death, for it has already excluded him.

Admittedly, the problem of lying cannot be solved by handing out truth like pills. The truth itself can have a disturbing and an isolating effect especially within the context of a system oriented rather exclusively to cure at the expense of genuine care. The doctor's reticence to discuss the subject cannot be written off solely as a problem of his own excessive fear of death or his own over-sensitive professional self-esteem. He has seen too many people avoid the question or ask the question without being certain that they really wanted an answer. The sacral dimensions of death are too awesome to admit of easy solution.

And yet there may be ways in which people can reach out to one another in word and action before the overwhelming event of death. It would be pretentious to outline these ways since they are not given to us fully except in the concrete case. Nevertheless, it may be possible to clear the ground of certain difficulties we face in maintaining solidarity in both *word* and *deed*. To do so, we need to return to our baseline in the interpretation of death as a sacred event.

The problem of words. Perhaps we are especially inhibited in words with the dying because our alternatives in language seem so poor. There are several types of discourse available to us: (1) direct, immediate, blunt talk; (2) circumlocution or doubletalk; (3) silence (which can be, of course, a mode of sharing, but oftentimes, a way of evading); and (4) discourse that proceeds by way of indirection.

Too often we assume (especially as Americans) that the only form of truth-telling is direct, immediate, blunt talk. Such talk seems to be the only alternative to evasive silence or circumlocution. On the subject of sex, for example, we assume that the only alternative to the repressions of a Victorian age is the tiresome, gabby, explicit discussion of sex imposed upon our adolescents from junior high onward.

There is, however, such a thing as *indirect* discourse on the subject of love and death. Obviously, gabby bluntness in the presence of one dying is wholly inappropriate. It reckons in no way with the solemnity of the event. To advocate the discussion of diagnosis or prognosis with every patient in clinical detail may be foolhardy. But the alternative to blunt talk need not be double-talk, a condescending cheerfulness, or a frightening silence.

Perhaps examples of what I mean by indirection will suffice. One doctor reports [11] that many patients instinctively brought up the question of their own death in an indirect form: some asked him, for example, whether he thought they should buy a house, marry, or undergo plastic surgery. The doctor realized that the answer, "yes—surely, go ahead—" in a big cheerful voice was an evasion. Meanwhile, the answer "No" was too curt—a reply which would have made further discussion impossible. He found it important to tell them simply that he recognized the importance of the question. From that point on, it was possible to discuss their uncertainties, anxieties and fears. Some kind of sharing could take place. It was not necessary to dwell on the subject for long. After its acknowledgment, it was possible to proceed to the details of daily life without the change of subject seeming an evasion.

Indirection may be achieved in another way. Although it sometimes may be too overbearing to approach the subject

[11] Samuel L. Feder, M.D., "Attitudes of Patients with Advanced Malignancy," *Ibid.,* p. 619.

frontally under the immediate pressure of its presence, a kind of indirection can be achieved if death is discussed in advance of a crisis. The rabbi, priest, or minister who suddenly feels like a tongue-tied irrelevancy in the sick room gets what he deserves if he has not worked through the problem with his people in a series of sermons or in work sessions with lay groups. Words too blunt and inappropriate in the crisis itself may, if spoken earlier, provide an indirect basis for sharing burdens.

The language of indirection is appropriate because, as has been argued throughout, death is a sacred event. For the most part, toward the sacred, the most fitting relation is indirect. The Jew did not attempt to look directly on Jahweh's face. A direct, immediate, casual confrontation was impossible. But avoidance of God's presence was not the only alternative. It was given to the Jew to hold his ground before his Lord in a relation that was genuine but indirect. So also, it is not necessary to dwell directly on the subject of death interminably or to avoid it by a condescending cheerfulness wholly inappropriate to the event. It may be possible, however, for two human beings to acknowledge death, be it ever so indirectly, and to hold their ground before it until they are parted.

The problem of action. In extremity, deeds are no easier to come by than words. Everyone grows uneasy. When nothing is left to be done, a man is inclined to pay his respects, look at his watch, and fish out an excuse that fetches him home. Perhaps, however, our discomfort is worsened by a concept of action somewhat inappropriate to overwhelming events. T. S. Eliot once said, there are two types of problems we face in life. In one case, the appropriate question is, what are we going to do about it? In the other case, the only fitting question is, how do we behave toward it? The deeper problems in life are of the latter kind. In the helping professions, the dividing line between these two questions falls roughly between the more glamorous systems of cure and the humbler action of care.

But unfortunately, as Americans (given philosophically to pragmatism and culturally to technology) and especially as Americans in those professions that get tinged with a messianic pretension, we are used to tackling problems in terms of the first question; and we are bereft when that question is inappropriate to the crisis. If all we can say is, what are we going to do about it?—then dying indeed (and our own death as well) is even more intensively a blow to professional self-esteem. But this is not the only question we need to ask. The question remains as to our mode of behavior toward an event which that behavior admittedly will not successfully dissolve. In extremity, it may not be possible to do something about a tragedy, but this inability need not altogether disable us humanly before it. Members of the helping professions belong to a network of care and not simply to an apparatus for cure.

The assumption made in this final discussion of words and deeds is that the trauma of dying need not mean the total eclipse of the human. To be sure, death "exposes" a man in the literal sense that it places him out in the open without shelter (like Hector facing Achilles outside the city gates). Furthermore, it "exposes" a man, his culture, and the helping professions in the sense that it reveals them in all their glaring inadequacies. But, finally, death can "expose" in the sense that it brings a man and his community out of concealment into unconcealment. It can test a man in such a way as to exhibit his manhood and test the community in such a way as to exhibit its humanity.

The ancient Greek and the modern existentialist are particularly concerned with the first sort of testing. Dying is a man's moment of glory in the literal sense of the Greek term, *doxa,* his "shining forth." Hector appears as a man, he steps forth into unconcealment in the course of his death. So also the solitary hero of the existentialist tradition is fully exhibited in his project toward death. But a culture with its roots in the Jewish and Christian traditions ought equally to be concerned with the second kind of testing: death as that occasion in which the community, wholly divested of messianic pretension, is revealed in its humanity as a network of care.

If our humanity is tested and revealed in the way in which we behave toward death; by the same token, it is obscured and diminished when death is concealed from view—when the dying are forced to make their exit anonymously, their ending unwitnessed, uncherished, unsuffered, and unrecorded except in the hospital files. So repressed indeed has the event of death been in our culture that when the dying man is rediscovered, he makes his entrance not as a hero, warrior, or martyr, but as a pedagogue. The subtitle to that recent book on death and dying by Dr. Elisabeth Kubler-Ross is, "What the dying have to *teach* doctors, nurses, clergy, and their own families." [12] Astonishingly enough, nurses, social workers, doctors, and theologians gather in seminars conducted by the dying. To each his own *dernière classe*.

When the community fails to declare itself to the dying, let the dying be brave enough to bear witness to the community, to remind the community of its own diminished life.

[12] Elisabeth Kubler-Ross, M.D., *On Death and Dying*, New York (The Macmillan Company, 1969). Italics mine.

(This essay is an expansion of a paper read for a symposium on death and dying sponsored by the Institute for Society, Ethics, and the Life Sciences, at the December 1971 meeting of The American Association for the Advancement of Science. Limited portions of the first and third sections of the paper were developed in an earlier draft for a symposium at Vanderbilt University, the proceedings of which were published by Abingdon Press under the title, *Perspectives on Death*.)

DEATH IN THE JUDAIC AND CHRISTIAN TRADITIONS

BY A. ROY ECKARDT

THE complexities of our topic arise, *inter alia,* from two major, paradoxical considerations, the one historical and the other dogmatic.

1. As the plural word "traditions" indicates, we are confronted, on the one hand, by discrete ideologies that have developed in contradistinctive ways over lengthy periods of time.[1] On the other hand, the two faith-traditions sustain many elements of continuity and mutuality, as becomes readily apparent when Western religious history is contrasted with non-Western. Our problem is further complicated by the fact, obvious to all, that neither the Judaic tradition nor the Christian tradition is monolithic, nor has either one remained unaffected by external influences.

2. The twofold declaration is made *(a)* that human beings are penetrated by mortality, that death stands arrayed as the conqueror and ineluctable end *(finis)* of individual human life,[2] and yet, *(b)* that death is not the end, either as *finis* or as *telos* (purpose, goal). Dissenters from the Judaic-Christian tradition— at this juncture we are permitted to speak of a single "tradition" —may discern in propositions *(a)* and *(b)* a foolish contradiction. The Jewish or Christian believer, on the contrary, receives the

---

[1] Arthur A. Cohen argues compellingly that "the conception of a Judeo-Christian tradition is mythological or, rather, not precisely mythological but ideological and hence, as in all ideologies, shot through with falsification, distortion, and untruth" in *The Myth of the Judeo-Christian Tradition* (New York: Schocken Books, 1971), p. ix.

[2] The coming death of all human life, generic as well as individual, is simply a matter of time, scientifically (i.e., ecologically) speaking. However, the difference between unnumbered individual deaths and the much more indeterminate, future demise of all humanity is elementary. It finds a counterpart in the dogmatic distinction between individual fate and collective fate, with correspondingly separate emphases respecting the outreach of divine judgment.

twin assertions as a constituent paradox of faith. *Finis* is indeed the nemesis of *telos*.[3] But death will be subjected to an eschatological power greater than itself. The divine *telos* must gain the final victory over *finis*.

I

We may not turn our backs upon shared human experiences all over the world—e.g., the universality of grief over the loss of loved ones—experiences that in a real sense stand in judgment upon every religious ideology. The emphasis within both Judaism and Christianity upon the *Einmaligkeit* (once-for-allness) of human death—and, accordingly, upon the once-for-allness of individual, finite lifespans—may seem to comprise a mere truism. After all, in the fabled little old lady's words, "very few people leave this world alive." The knowledge that life ends in the grave is, as such, human rather than religious. In this respect there is nothing original in the Judaic-Christian emphasis upon the reality and fatefulness of death. However, it must be noted that a common-sense, experiential orientation has not always agreed that death is *finis*. For example, the (reputed) communication between departed spirits and the living has been called upon as proof that men may survive death and bodily decay. Spiritualism, at least of the Anglo-Saxon variety, claims to involve as much a form of empirical knowledge, in the scientific sense, as a practical religion.[4] Nevertheless, the Judaic-Christian traditions, comprehended in their originally normative, biblical forms, have exerted weighty socio-religious influence here through their insistence that to die is to die. And if the dead are really dead, there is no way to reach them or for them to communicate with us.[5]

[3] Cf. Reinhold Niebuhr, *The Nature and Destiny of Man* (New York: Charles Scribner's Sons, 1943), Vol. II, p. 287.

[4] Pierre Nordon, *Conan Doyle* (London: John Murray, 1966), p. 141.

[5] It is, of course, true that some Christians have made spiritualist claims. A recent case is the late Bishop James A. Pike.

The intellectual and social impact of the Judaic-Christian anthropology of death comes into much sharper relief when our frame of reference extends to the world religions and world cultures. The domain of authentic religious controversy is now entered. We think of Hinduism and Buddhism, according to whose central traditions "the present life of each person is only one of an infinite series of lives, past and to come." [6] Of course, the Judaic-Christian affirmation of an afterlife shows that the Western tradition [7] and the Hindu-Buddhist tradition are not *in toto* disparate. Nevertheless, the normative viewpoints, as between much of Asia and the West, differ markedly. The assertion of death as *finis*, as an existentially fateful happening qualitatively other than just one more ultimately inconsequential transition from temporal life to temporal life, lies deep within the Judaic-Christian outlook.

II

The doctrinal insistence upon human mortality is grounded in the theological anthropology of the Tanakh, the Hebrew Bible. In direct contrast to the later Greek dualism, which declared an antithesis between mortal body and immortal soul, Hebraic anthropology construes man as a psychophysical unity that expresses itself in different qualities. "Man's personality is always identified with the animated body; hence it is always conceived as an

---

[6] S. G. F. Brandon, *The Judgment of the Dead: The Idea of Life After Death in the Major Religions* (New York: Charles Scribner's Sons, 1967), p. 165. However, the Hindu-Buddhist tradition itself admits of exceptions. The Vedic literature, which was to become the sacred literature of Hinduism, allows for an alternative eschatology: individual life terminates at death and cannot be repeated (*ibid.*, p. 168). As in the case of the Judaic and Christian traditions, Hinduism and Buddhism have markedly diverged from each other. One essential difference centers in traditional Hinduism's affirmation of the soul (*atman*), in contrast to the teaching of the unreality of the soul (*anatta*) in Buddhism, which began as a reform movement within Hinduism.

[7] Islam here carries forward the Judaic-Christian tradition and is in this respect "Western."

indivisible organism functioning as an integrated unity. . . ." [8]
The Hebrew *nephesh* and the Greek *psyche,* though often translated as "soul," are, in the biblical documents, frequently better
translated as "living person" or as "self." The word "self" is
the nearest that an English concept can come to a comprehensive
rendering of the Hebrew and Greek terms. Generally speaking,
these terms are not used in the sense of some kind of immortal
soul.[9]

Even if man is set apart from the rest of creation—he is
fashioned "in the image" of God (Gen. 1:26–7)—he is still a
mortal creature, formed "from the dust of the ground" and
destined to return to that place. "Dust you are, to dust you shall
return" (Gen. 2:7, 3:19).[10] When the spirit of God (*ruach;* cf.
Greek, *pneuma*) is taken away, man is no more. The Book of
Job is quite categorical:

> But man dies, and is laid low;
>   man breathes his last, and where is he?
> As waters fail from a lake,
>   and a river wastes away and dries up,
> So man lies down and rises not again;
>   till the heavens are no more he will not awake,
>   or be roused out of his sleep (14:10–12).

And the Psalmist laments:

> Thou dost sweep men away; they are like a dream,
>   like grass which is renewed in the morning:
> in the morning it flourishes and is renewed;
>   in the evening it fades and withers. . . .
> For all our days pass away under thy wrath,
>   our years come to an end like a sigh.

8 Harold Knight, *The Hebrew Prophetic Consciousness* (London: Lutterworth
Press, 1947), p. 125.

9 See Millar Burrows, *An Outline of Biblical Theology* (Philadelphia: The Westminster Press, 1946), pp. 134–136, 138.

10 The divine sentencing of Adam to "return to the ground" comes, it is true,
after "the fall" (Gen. 3:1 ff.). Some biblical literalists have argued (often by reference to Gen. 3:22) that man would, therefore, have been spared death had he not
been disobedient to God. This claim is unsupported in the Bible as a whole.

The years of our life are threescore and ten,
   or even by reason of strength fourscore;
yet their span is but toil and trouble;
   they are soon gone, and we fly away (90:5–6, 9–10).

In the New Testament, the Book of James carries forward the traditional, normative interpretation: "Come now, you who say, 'Today or tomorrow we will go into such and such a town and spend a year there and trade and get gain'; whereas you do not know about tomorrow. What is your life? For you are a mist that appears for a little time and then vanishes" (4:13–14).

The theological-anthropological outlook of the New Testament is overwhelmingly determined by the affirmation of the raising from the dead of Jesus as the Christ. Thus, from the beginning death and its sequel was a central question in the Christian *Weltanschauung*. The event of Jesus' resurrection is believed to open the way to resurrection and eternal life for other men. It is held to disclose God's eschatological power over death and the grave: "The last enemy to be destroyed is death. . . . O Death, where is your victory? O Death, where is your sting?" (I Cor. 15:26, 55.) The dogma of Jesus' resurrection constitutes the primordial separation between the Jewish and Christian faiths. Nevertheless, that dogma does not alter in the slightest the nature of biblical anthropology as such. It in no way subverts the recognition of human mortality. In direct contrast to the heresy of docetism, which claimed that since Jesus was divine and immortal, he merely *seemed* (Greek, *dokeo*) to die, the New Testament insists that his death was real, constituting the same *finis* that awaits all men, although in his case a terrible one: "And at the ninth hour Jesus cried with a loud voice, 'Elo-i, Elo-i, lama sabachthani?' which means, 'My God, my God, why hast thou forsaken me?' . . . And Jesus uttered a loud cry and breathed his last" (Mark 15:34, 36; cf. Job 14:10, cited above).

There is no basis for any judgment that the New Testament evangelists took a viewpoint different from the Hebraic anthropology they inherited. This observation applies to Paul of Tarsus as much as to anyone. The Pauline distinction in I Corinthians 15 between the earthly, perishable body and the heavenly, spiritual body has nothing to do with the Greek philosophical idea of the immortality of the soul.[11] In Pauline thought, "body" (*soma*) refers to the total personality. Hence, for Paul "the only possible form which human life in any true and proper sense may take here or hereafter is 'somatic.' "[12] Paul is affirming the power of God to bring life out of death. The term "resurrection of the person" may help to offset the ambiguity in the expression "resurrection of the body." Paul explicitly maintains that the body that is sown "is not the body that shall be" (vs. 37). It is from this point of view that we may speak of the "resurrection of the dead." (The theological context of Paul's analysis in I Corinthians 15 is the resurrection of Jesus. Thus, it is evident that Paul meant to apply the foregoing distinctions to the event of Jesus' resurrection, which involved anything but a soul-like apparition and yet presumably transcended the body that was "sown.")

III

Where life is considered a divine gift, death and other adversities are received within that same frame of reference.

Religious martyrdom has been honored in the Judaic tradition. Normatively speaking, the Jew is obliged in the event of persecution to submit to martyrdom rather than to betray his faith. Such a free, responsible act is identified as *kiddush ha-Shem*, the sanctifying or hallowing of the name of God. Still today a Sabbath prayer is said for "the holy congregations who laid down their lives for the sanctification of the divine name." We must beware of simplistic conclusions that tempt to immorality. As

11 Rudolf Bultmann, *Theology of the New Testament* (New York: Charles Scribner's Sons, 1951), Vol. I, pp. 203, 345–346.

12 James J. Heller, "The Resurrection of Man," *Theology Today*, XV, 2 (July, 1958), p. 222.

Emil L. Fackenheim points out, the Nazi holocaust had no precedent in previous Jewish history. He emphasizes that past martyrs died for their faith, but Hitler and his cohorts murdered Jews simply on account of their "race." [13] Across the centuries of the church, the Christian martyr has also been celebrated. One contemporary source describes martyrdom as "the fullest proof of love. By martyrdom a disciple is transformed into an image of his Master by freely accepting death for the salvation of the world. . . ." [14]

Let us turn to the specific event of death. Jewish funeral services usually include the words from the Book of Job: "The Lord has given; the Lord has taken away; blessed be the name of the Lord" (1:21). And yet, in the Judaic and Christian traditions religious resignation to death is heavily qualified, *ante diem*. Those who unwarrantedly take human life are condemned: "You shall not commit murder" (Exod. 20:13). And the death of children is opposed: "it is not the will of my father who is in heaven that one of these little ones should perish" (Matt. 18:14). On the other hand, death is sometimes interpreted as divine judgment: "the perverseness of transgressors shall destroy them . . . but uprightness safeguards against death" (Prov. 11:3, 4); "the wages of sin is death . . . Rom. 6:23).[15] However, this understanding is also subject to qualification. Most Jews today, together with many Christians, consider wantonly immoral the claim that the Jews who were put to death in the Nazi concentration camps were being "punished" by God.

In Judaism an individual confessional is said at the approach of death: ". . . if my death be fully determined by Thee, I will

13 Emil L. Fackenheim, *God's Presence in History* (New York: New York University Press, 1970), p. 69.

14 Vatican Council II, "Dogmatic Constitution on the Church," 42, cited in *The Catechism of Modern Man (All in the Words of Vatican II and Related Documents)* (Boston: St. Paul Editions, 1968), p. 108.

15 St. Paul may have subscribed to that aspect of rabbinic teaching which regarded death as a consequence of Adam's sin. The notion that human sin was the cause of death did become widespread in orthodox Christianity, as exemplified in the fourth-century churchman Athanasius (Reinhold Niebuhr, *op. cit.*, Vol. I, pp. 174–176).

accept it in love from thy hand. May my death be an atonement for all the sins . . . of which I have been guilty toward Thee. . . . O Father of the fatherless, protect my beloved kinfolk with whose souls my own is knit. . . . Amen, amen." In his final conscious moments the Jew recites the *shema*: "Hear, O Israel, the Lord is our God, the Lord is one."

Utter simplicity characterizes Judaic burial practices. The plain shroud dates back to the second century C.E. when it was used for the poor. That all men are equal in death is further symbolized by the plain wood coffin (dispensed with in Israel and some Eastern lands). Interment takes place as quickly as possible: Death is death. Yet every respect must be shown to the body. Autopsies are permitted only on the ground of specific evidence of the fostering of human welfare through medical and scientific advance. Cremation is forbidden in the tradition, although it is practiced today by some Reform Jews. The body is placed in the ground or in a sepulcher.

Traditionally, funeral services have usually been held in the home of the deceased. The rites include readings from the Psalms and conclude with a prayer for the peace of the soul of the departed. During the ensuing seven days the mourners remain quietly at home. Visitors console them with such words as: "May the Almighty comfort you together with those who mourn for Zion and Jerusalem." Throughout a virtual year of mourning the loved ones periodically recite the distinctive *Kaddish*: "Magnified and sanctified be the name of the Lord in the world which he hath created according to his will. May he establish his kingdom in your life-time and in your days, and in the life-time of all the house of Israel, speedily and at a near time. . . ." It is often noted that the *Kaddish* makes no mention of death or the dead; God and the praise of God are the focus. Before year's end a memorial stone is erected and a ceremony takes place at the grave. The anniversary of the death of the departed (*Yahrzeit*) is observed through the reciting of a prayer and the lighting of a candle. At the synagogue those who have lost close relatives say special memorial prayers (*Yizkor*) after the anniversary. This is done on the Day of Atonement, and on the last days of Passover, Sukkot, and Shevuot.

The Judaic rites of burial and mourning at once provide expression for grief, strengthen family and community solidarity, honor God, and inculcate acceptance of his will. These values have also been carried forward within the Christian tradition. In Catholicism one sacrament, Extreme Unction, is made specifically available, as offering strength and grace to the soul and, hopefully, even health to the body, for baptized, responsible persons who are in danger of death from illness, accident, or old age. (Under emergency conditions and in special circumstances priests may administer this sacrament to "separated brothers." [16]) Whenever possible the Sacrament of Penance is administered first. If this is not possible, Extreme Unction [17] is held to effect the remission of sins, on the condition that the recipient is in "good dispositions" or was so before losing consciousness. Faithful who are in danger of death are required to receive Holy Communion.

On or before the day of burial the body is taken to the church for the Office and Mass of the Dead. Christian burial is ordinarily withheld from, among others, a suicide (*felo de se*) and those who had directed that their body be cremated. Cremation is strictly forbidden in Catholicism, "which enjoins burial of the body out of reverence to what was in life the temple of the Holy Ghost. . . ." However, cremation is not *ipso facto* wrong and may be permitted by ecclesiastical authorities for such a grave reason as public health. Euthanasia, defined as "the direct and deliberate painless killing, or hastening of the death of, one in great pain," is considered murder, "which nothing can excuse." [18] Among the Protestant denominations there is

---

16 "Directory on Ecumenism," 55, cited in *The Catechism of Modern Man, op. cit.*, p. 195.

17 The symbol "extreme" derives not from the idea of preparation for death, but from the fact that the anointing with oil follows temporally after anointings at Baptism, Confirmation, and Holy Orders.

18 *A Catholic Dictionary*, ed. by D. Attwater, 2d rev. ed. (New York: The Mac-

disagreement over the practices of cremation and euthanasia, with increasing degrees of acceptance on both points.

The offering of prayers for the help of the dead in Purgatory is very firmly established in Catholicism and equally firmly denied in Protestantism. In the Episcopal Church special prayers are said during visitation to the sick, as exemplified in these words from the *Book of Common Prayer*: "O Lord, look down from heaven, behold, visit, and relieve this thy servant. Look upon (him/her) with the eyes of thy mercy, give (him/her) comfort and sure confidence in thee, defend (him/her) from the danger of the enemy, and keep (him/her) in perpetual peace and safety; through Jesus Christ our Lord." Parallel prayers and rites are found in various Protestant communions. The Order for the Burial of the Dead in the United Methodist Church combines the reading of a number of appropriate biblical passages with such prayers as this: "O God, the Lord of life, the Conqueror of death, our help in every time of trouble, who dost not willingly grieve or afflict the children of men; comfort us who mourn, and give us grace, in the presence of death, to worship thee, that we may have sure hope of eternal life and be enabled to put our whole trust in thy goodness and mercy; through Jesus Christ our Lord." The *Book of Common Prayer* stipulates that as earth is "cast upon the Body by some standing by," the officiant says:

Forasmuch as it hath pleased Almighty God, in his wise providence to take out of this world the soul of our deceased (brother/sister), we therefore commit (his/her) body to the ground; earth to earth, ashes to ashes, dust to dust; looking for the general Resurrection in the last day, and the life of the world to come, through our Lord Jesus Christ; at whose second coming in glorious majesty to judge the world, the earth and the sea shall give up their dead; and the corruptible bodies of those who sleep in him shall be changed, and made like unto his own glorious body; according to the mighty working whereby he is able to subdue all things unto himself.

millan Company, 1953), pp. 128, 179; "Pastoral Constitution on the Church in the Modern World," 27, cited in *The Catechism of Modern Man,* p. 547. Abortion is also held to be murder.

The more desacralized and secularized a society becomes, the less it is possible to implement theological understandings and norms.   However, certain minimal questions may be put from a Judaic-Christian point of view: To what extent do funeral and burial practices in a given society acknowledge that death is real? And to what extent do they honor "this life," the events of time and place?

There is no way to predict with any degree of certainty the impact that the newer medical technology will eventually have upon the Judaic and Christian traditions.   Examples include prostheses and organ transplants. Some human bodies are now being frozen at death, in the hope of resuscitation with the aid of tomorrow's scientific remedies. Any indefinite prolongation of individual human life raises fundamental moral issues for both traditions, including the question of the uninhabitability of planet Earth due to overpopulation. Every generation has a moral responsibility to unborn generations.

IV

In their understanding of man as a creature of nature who nevertheless transcends nature in freedom and imagination, our traditions emphasize the uniqueness of the human fear of death, in contrast to other animals.[19]   This fear is one essential root of the question, "if a man die, will he live again?" (Job 14:14). In the words of the Second Vatican Council, man "rebels against death because he bears in himself an eternal seed which cannot be reduced to sheer matter." [20]   A man of perfect faith would neither fear death nor be exercised over his mortality. But most men, in their pride and unbelief, hardly anticipate their demise with equanimity.[21]

19 Niebuhr, *op. cit.*, Vol. I, pp. 98–99.
20 "Pastoral Constitution on the Church in the Modern World," 18, cited in *The Catechism of Modern Man*, p. 137.
21 Niebuhr, *op. cit.*, Vol. I, p. 174.

Since our subject is death rather than life after death, it might be objected that we ought to lay aside the latter question. Yet just as human life is conditioned by the stern eventuality of death, so the possibility or impossibility of an afterlife must influence our whole understanding of and attitude toward death itself. It is clear that the belief in immortality of the soul will sustain a vastly different orientation and response to the event of death than will a belief in human mortality. Reactions to the latter belief will in turn differ, depending upon an affirmation or denial of a divinely-wrought resurrection.

Ezekiel, prophet of the Babylonian Exile, describes a valley of dry bones, "the whole house of Israel." God will cause breath to enter them, will endow them with sinews, flesh, and skin, and they "shall live." "Thus says the Lord God: 'Behold, I will open your graves, and raise you from your graves, . . . and I will bring you home into the land of Israel' " (37:1–12).

During the period of the Second Temple, a developing feature of Jewish eschatological and messianic ideas was the linking of universality, national hope, and individuality. At the "last day" judgment will be meted out to all nations, including Israel. From the second century B.C.E. the expectation of a final, universal judgment, understood in primarily collective terms, had become a constituent element in the Jewish outlook. But the longings of the individual were also given voice through the doctrine of the resurrection of the dead, which from rabbinic times became a fundamental Judaic doctrine.[22] In the period of the Maccabees the prophet Daniel foresaw the awakening of the dead, "some to everlasting life, and some to shame and everlasting contempt" (12:2). The Pharisees believed in this idea of resurrection; the Sadducees rejected it.

The rise of Christianity carried forward the above develop-

[22] Brandon, *op. cit.*, pp. 70, 71; Yehoshua Guttman and Menahem Stern, "From the Babylonian Exile to the Bar Kochba Revolt," in *The Jews in their Land,* ed. by D. Ben-Gurion (Garden City, N. Y.: Doubleday & Co., 1966), p. 154; *The Encyclopedia of the Jewish Religion,* ed. by R. J. Z. Werblowsky and G. Wigoder (New York: Holt, Rinehart and Winston, 1965), p. 331.

ments but sought to subject Jewish universalist and individualist expectations to Christian dogmatic understandings, including the eclipse of Israel's national hopes. The doctrine of resurrection was more and more assimilated to the doctrine of divine judgment, through the teaching that the good are raised for God's reward and the evil are raised for his punishment. The "judgment of the dead" has ever been basic and integral to Christian theology.[23]

The scriptural insistence upon death as man's fate-destiny (*Bestimmung*) could not prevent the incursion into our two traditions of the essentially Greek idea of "immortality of the soul." The doctrines of resurrection and immortality were brought together. While the encounter had to be a mutually uncomfortable one, it could take place by virtue of a shared witness that *finis* is not the last word respecting death. The teaching of divine judgment helped provide the rationale of the meeting. For no great sophistication is needed to see the force of the question: How can the dead be judged when they are, after all, dead?

The meeting was given additional, specific impetus by the assumption, present within the biblical period itself, of some kind of quasi-survival after the event of death (an assumption that is hardly reconcilable logically with death as total extinction). The reference is to Sheol, where the spirits of the dead—whether righteous or unrighteous—allegedly endured a kind of shadowy and gloomy existence (cf. Job 3:17–19; Isa. 14:9–11; Ezek. 32:17–32). However, with the coming of belief in resurrection, Sheol became a temporary abode of the dead, a waiting place for the future judgment.[24] In the New Testament the corresponding representation is "Hades" (cf. Matt. 11:23; 16:18; Luke 16:19–31; and the Apostles' Creed, according to which Jesus Christ "descended into hell" or "the place of departed spirits").

A major positive reason why our two traditions could become

23 Brandon, *op. cit.*, p. 98.
24 Burrows, *op. cit.*, p. 194; Brandon, *op. cit.*, p. 68.

vulnerable to the idea of immortality is that the very dogma of post-mortem, divine retribution disallows death as the absolutely final episode in human life. (Of course, the normative contention persisted that the raising of the dead is the instrumentality for the ultimate divine reckoning with wrong—and with right.) However, from the standpoint of immortality, death appears primarily as a form of liberation—a consequence not totally unlike that provided by death as unconditional *finis*. From the standpoint of resurrection, liberation is not denied but it is overshadowed by such affirmations as the Kingship of God, the world-to-come (Hebrew, *olam ha-ba*), the messianic age, Heaven, Hell, eternal life, and—most crucial in our context—the judgment of the dead. (To stay dead—*contra* the Judaic-Christian tradition—may be a bane *vis-à-vis* Heaven but it is a blessing *vis-à-vis* Hell. Divine judgment can entail bliss as much as adversity. The hope of Heaven mortifies death; the fear of Hell prospers it. Relative to Heaven, death is not a final evil; relative to Hell, it is a specter. We have, then, a kind of vertical scale extending from hope to hopelessness: Heaven; death devoid of any sequel; Hell.)

V

In the history of Christian thought one prevalent resolution of the conflict between resurrection and immortality, and accordingly of the evident contradiction between death as *finis* and a continuation beyond death, was the assimilating of the idea of immortality to an intermediate state and the applying of the idea of resurrection to the end (*eschaton*), God's final consummation and judgment. This understanding was also set forth within Jewish theology.[25] Immortality, i.e., abidingness, came to function, so to say, as an intellectually needful link between the *Einmaligkeit* of death and the resurrection, the ultimate divine fulfillment.

[25] Burrows, *op. cit.*, p. 194.

There could also develop the medieval teaching of Purgatory, which, in a manner of speaking, moved ahead the process of divine judgment in limited but fear-inspiring fashion by imposing suffering, punishment, and cleansing upon "the souls there detained" (Council of Trent) between the times of the "particular judgment" of the individual at death and the "general judgment" following the "general resurrection" at the "last day." [26]

Although Judaism developed no dogma of Purgatory in the Catholic Christian sense,[27] by rabbinic times a man was already held to receive, upon death, reward and punishment for the manner of his life. However, this understanding was supplemented, and in some measure transcended, through the doctrine of the *olam ha-ba*, the future age, which "is everlasting and wholly good" and which involves "reward for good deeds in this world." Jewish thinkers in the Middle Ages fully subscribed to the teaching of eschatological retribution.[28]

It is a highly moot question whether the *olam ha-ba* is to be construed as a transformed state of this world-time or as "wholly-other" blessedness.[29]   It is obvious, in any event, that the Judaic tradition is faced with the same intellectual-eschatological challenge that confronts the Christian tradition: the great tension between proximity and ultimacy.   As Professor Brandon points

[26] Catholic theology also formulated the idea of Limbo, the portion for virtuous souls who died before the saving event of Christ, and a *limbus infantium*, for infants who died before baptism and would be deprived of the Beatific Vision, yet be without torment (Brandon, *op. cit.*, pp. 115, 116).

[27] Rabbi Louis Finkelstein refers, however, to "many rabbinic authorities" who hold that certain people may obtain immortal life after undergoing temporary suffering for their sins after death. He cites the Talmudic verse, "the punishment of the wicked in Gehenna does not exceed twelve months" in "The Beliefs and Practices of Judaism," *The Religions of Democracy* (New York: The Devin-Adair Company, 1949), p. 24.

[28] *The Encyclopedia of the Jewish Religion, op. cit.*, pp. 109, 332. However, the rabbis emphasized that neither the expectation of reward nor the fear of punishment is a legitimate primary motive for virtue. Antigonus of Sokho, one of the founders of rabbinic Judaism, wrote: "Be not as servants that serve their Master with a thought of obtaining reward; but be as servants that serve their Master without thought of obtaining reward" (cf. Jesus of Nazareth in Matt. 5:43–48).

[29] *The Encyclopedia of the Jewish Religion*, pp. 289–90.

out, the Protestant Reformers, by repudiating the idea of Purgatory (while remaining convinced of divine judgment, Heaven, and Hell [30]), landed themselves in the very difficulty that Purgatory had been calculated to solve: how to account for the fate of individuals from the time of their death until the Last Judgment. Certain Anabaptists held that men's souls simply slept in the intervening time and were finally resurrected in their bodies.[31] But this constituted a tacit endorsement of the idea of immortality: after all, a soul asleep is no less a soul. The undeniable, ultimate destruction of a human being's "remains" (*nota bene*) presents the additional, formidable complication: What does it mean to speak of resurrection "in one's body?" As a matter of fact, it was partly in reaction to literalistic understandings of "resurrection of the body" that "immortality of the soul" could become a more acceptable way of expressing the conviction of life after death.[32]   One persistent effort to meet the difficulty calls upon the Pauline distinction, alluded to above, between the perishable, physical body that "is sown" and the imperishable, spiritual body that "is raised."

Judaism has not been beset by the measure of eschatological controversy that has plagued the Christian churches. For one thing, in the Judaic tradition much less emphasis falls upon belief—even where "belief" is construed in an extra-intellectual way. (The term "orthodoxy" applied to Judaism is in a strictly derivational sense misleading; an accurate term is "orthopraxy," right behavior.)   Any such notion as believing "in the Lord Jesus

[30] "The souls of the righteous being then made perfect in holiness, are received into the highest heavens, where they behold the face of God in light and glory, waiting for the full redemption of their bodies; and the souls of the wicked are cast into hell, where they remain in torments and utter darkness, reserved to the judgment of the great day. Besides these two places for souls separated from their bodies, the Scripture acknowledgeth none" (*The Westminster Confession of Faith*, XXXII, 1).

[31] Brandon, *op. cit.*, p. 132.

[32] Robert McAfee Brown, "Immortality," in *A Handbook of Christian Theology*, ed. by M. Halverson and A. A. Cohen (Cleveland: The World Publishing Company, 1958), p. 184.

Christ" in order to "be saved" (cf. Acts 16:31) is totally foreign to the Judaic tradition and, indeed, repugnant to it. Of direct theological relevance here is the consideration that the Christian faith embodies a "realized eschatology" (to adapt C. H. Dodd's expression), in contrast to the open and unrealized eschatology of Judaism. Historically, Christianity has concentrated much more upon the fate of the dead—a conspicuous modern exception is Protestant Liberalism—and it has been much more tempted to "know the geography of heaven and hell, and the furniture of the one and the temperature of the other." [33] Judaism's more reserved and even agnostic outlook has made for a certain tolerance, in contradistinction to Christianity.

There are grounds for a hypothesis that the reluctance of Jewish thought to erect a detailed structure of eschatological rewards and punishments (in marked contrast to the Jewish achievement of a moral and legal corpus respecting obligations in this world) stems in part from a refusal, in conscience, to fall into the vanities of the Gentiles (cf. Matt. 10:5), namely, Christendom. This conjecture gains persuasiveness when we bear in mind that in terms both of intensity and of duration, the eschatological fabrications of the church have meant death and destruction for no people so much as for the Jews. By making due allowance for the great impact upon Jews of these life-experiences, we are aided in resolving such a historical enigma as the following: The Last Judgment in the New Testament derives ultimately from the Jewish apocalyptic tradition,[34] and yet the Judaic tradition—even within the bounds of the people Israel—retreated from an eschatology resembling the Christian dogma. Did not the Jewish people feel upon their own backs the afflictions of a "realized eschatology?" This fact could help to spare them from comparable human temptations.

In the ongoing dialectic between Christianity and Judaism,

<hr/>

[33] Reinhold Niebuhr, *Discerning the Signs of the Times* (New York: Charles Scribner's Sons, 1946), p. 154.

[34] Brandon, *op. cit.*, p. 102 and *passim*.

the realized eschatology of the resurrection is counterbalanced by the perpetuity of God's people Israel. At this point, among others, the force of James Parkes' distinction between Judaism as directed to man as social being and Christianity as directed to man as personal being becomes apparent.[35] However, the distinction must not be overdrawn. The Christian tradition emphasizes the community of the redeemed. And the Judaic tradition certainly allows for the resurrection of the individual person: "What man shall live and not see death or save himself from the power of Sheol? . . . God will ransom my life, he will take me from the power of Sheol" (Pss. 89:48; 49:15).

VI

The Catholic Church early came under the influence of the Greek dichotomy of body and soul. The affirmation of an immortal soul gained a prevailing place in Catholic dogma, although not to the point of ousting the doctrine of resurrection. Rather, the attempt has been made to have a place for both ideas. The human person is comprehended in dual terms: man *has* a body and he *is* a soul. In fact, human death is defined as the departure of the soul. Since the soul does not die, there can be no resurrection for it. Nor is there any ground for supposing that the soul will ever perish, for "no reason can be given why God should annihilate it."[36] In one catechism, widely used for many years in Catholic secondary schools and colleges in the United States, we find a perfect expression of this dualistic viewpoint: "Man is a creature composed of body and soul. . . . Human souls live forever because they are spirits. . . . The never-ending life of the soul is called immortality. . . . By 'the resurrection of the body' is meant that at the end of the world the bodies of all men will rise from the earth and be united again to their souls, nevermore

---

[35] See the exposition of Parkes' views in A. Roy Eckardt, *Elder and Younger Brothers* (New York: Charles Scribner's Sons, 1967), pp. 82–89, especially pp. 83–84.
[36] *A Catholic Dictionary, op. cit.*, pp. 138, 246, 429.

to be separated." [37]   However, it is understood that the body, while it can be identified as the same body, will not have the same characteristics of material extension, will not be subject to sickness or death, and will not have the defects of an earthly body.[38]

The exigencies of historical development and the subtleties of linguistic change have been such that when many Christians and Jews speak of immortality they mean to convey the ideas of personal survival and "everlasting life," and they often imply a need to merit immortality in contrast to the Greek idea of immortality as an automatic, intrinsic attribute of man's nature.   Louis Finkelstein's interpretation of immortality as the "persistence of the human personality" in ultimate and endless communion with God, the "highest reward which man can attain," and the loss of which is the "greatest punishment he can suffer"—an understanding that Finkelstein holds to be that of "most Jewish theologians"—will find favor with many believers in resurrection.[39]

The relevance and force of any polemic against the teaching of immortality will vary with the meanings attached to "immortality" and "resurrection."   Thus the idea of "conditional immortality" need not be antithetical to the resurrection teaching, in contrast to "immortality" regarded as a natural human prerogative.   There is all the difference in the world between the hope that a personal "soul" may be enabled to endure beyond death and the claim that, upon death, an impersonal essence is merged once again with an impersonal Absolute.   The first understanding is not inconsistent with the "resurrection of the dead."   On the other hand, we cannot overestimate the influence of interpretations of immortality that appear to range themselves in opposition to the teaching of resurrection.

The renowned Jewish philosopher, Moses Maimonides (1135–

[37] *A Catechism of Christian Doctrine, Revised Edition of the Baltimore Catechism,* No. 3 (Paterson, N. J.: St. Anthony Guild Press, 1949), pp. 38, 40, 137.

[38] J. Elliot Ross, "The Roman Catholic Religion in Creed and Life," in *The Religions of Democracy, op. cit.,* p. 123.

[39] Finkelstein, *op. cit.,* p. 24.

1204) included the idea of resurrection as the last of his "Thirteen Principles," which are still reproduced in Hebrew prayer books: "I believe with perfect faith that there will be a resurrection of the dead at the time when it shall please the Creator, blessed be his name, and exalted be the remembrance of him for ever and ever." [40]   Here is an important instance, however, where "resurrection" was actually intended to mean "immortality." Maimonides stood in a tradition begun by the Jewish Platonist, Philo of Alexandria, (c. 25 B.C.E.–40 C.E.), for whom survival after death centered in the soul.   In his *Essay on the Resurrection of the Dead*, Maimonides explicitly rejected bodily survival and assigned the afterlife exclusively to the enjoyment of the soul.[41]

The influential "Pittsburgh Platform" of Reform Jewry (1885) went much farther than Maimonides and rejected the teaching of resurrection outright: "We reassert the doctrine of Judaism that the soul is immortal, grounding this belief on the divine nature of the human spirit, which forever finds bliss in righteousness and misery in wickedness.   We reject as ideas not rooted in Judaism, the beliefs both in bodily resurrection and in Gehenna and Eden (Hell and Paradise) as abodes for everlasting punishment and reward." [42]   It is certain that the framers of this statement would find wholly unacceptable any distinction between a body that is "sown" and a body that is "raised."   More decisive are their idealist-immanentist presuppositions, according to which man is hardly lower than the angels and is, indeed, "divine." The pronouncement is very far from the biblical awareness of man as dust that must return to dust.

There has been a tendency within Conservative Judaism to identify "resurrection" with "immortality of the soul."   Orthodox Jewish representatives have tended, by contrast, to retain the

---

40 A. Th. Philips, *Daily Prayers*, rev. edn. (New York: Hebrew Publishing Company, n.d.), p. 167.

41 Ben Zion Bokser, *Judaism: Profile of a Faith* (New York: Alfred A. Knopf, 1963), pp. 141–142.

42 From *The Jewish Encyclopedia*, ed. by I. Singer (New York: Funk and Wagnalls, 1907), Vol. IV, p. 215.

"resurrection of the body" in a literalist sense, while diverging from one another over the applicability of resurrection to all mankind, the Jewish people, or the righteous.[43]

In modern times the ascendancy of moral and philosophical idealism helped to reinforce claims to human immortality within Western religious thought. In Protestant Liberalism the teaching of immortality was proclaimed by, among many others, one of this country's most famous preachers, Harry Emerson Fosdick. His "modern use of the Bible" is typified in these words: "When . . . a man says, I believe in the immortality of the soul but not in the resurrection of the flesh, . . . only superficial dogmatism can deny that that man believes the Bible. It is precisely the thing at which the Bible was driving that he does believe." [44]

The doctrine of the "resurrection of the body" has caused serious problems for those Jewish (and Christian) thinkers whose theological outlook seeks to be purely "spiritual," and who cannot accept what is, for them, an unwarrantedly materialist eschatology.[45] The teaching of immortality has helped them to retain some form of eschatological faith without betraying their intellectual integrity.[46] Yet, if "the doctrine of the resurrection is what our age has been least able to believe," [47] the teaching of the immortality of the soul is not one whit less problematic. An irony in the rationalist viewpoint is that prevailing scientific understanding thinks of man as "a unified psychosomatic being in whom the physical and spiritual aspects of life are so closely inter-

---

[43] *The Encyclopedia of the Jewish Religion*, p. 331. Moses Maimonides advocated the last-mentioned alternative.

[44] Harry Emerson Fosdick, *The Modern Use of the Bible* (New York: The Macmillan Company, 1940), p. 129; see also his monograph *The Assurance of Immortality* (New York: Association Press, 1940).

[45] *The Encyclopedia of the Jewish Religion*, p. 331.

[46] For a brief and careful argument on the side of immortality of the soul from the perspective of the philosophy of religion, see D. Z. Phillips, *Death and Immortality* (London: Macmillan-St. Martin's Press, 1970). A recent analysis of death from both a philosophical and a Christian theological perspective, including a critique of the doctrine of immortality, is Helmut Thielicke's *Death and Life* (Philadelphia: Fortress Press, 1970).

[47] Frederick Sontag, *The God of Evil* (New York: Harper & Row, 1970), p. 59.

related, and indeed overlapping, that no separation of these elements is possible." [48]

VII

In recent years the doctrine of the resurrection of the dead has been reasserted within Christian and Jewish theological circles. In the thinking of Reinhold Niebuhr, the symbol of the "resurrection of the body" points to the unity of man as a creature of both nature and spirit.

> The hope of the resurrection . . . embodies the very genius of the Christian idea of the historical. On the one hand it implies that eternity will fulfill and not annul the richness and variety which the temporal process has elaborated. On the other it implies that the condition of finiteness and freedom, which lies at the basis of historical existence, is a problem for which there is no solution by any human power. Only God can solve this problem. . . .
>
> In this answer of faith the meaningfulness of history is the more certainly affirmed because the consummation of history as a human possibility is denied. The resurrection is not a human possibility in the sense that immortality of the soul is thought to be so. All the plausible and implausible proofs for the immortality of the soul are efforts on the part of the human mind to master and to control the consummation of life. They all try to prove in one way or another that an eternal element in the nature of man is worthy and capable of survival beyond death. But every mystic or rational technique which seeks to extricate the eternal element tends to deny the meaningfulness of the historical unity of body and soul; and with it the meaningfulness of the whole historical process with its infinite elaborations of that unity. . . .
>
> As against these conceptions of consummation in which man denies the significance of his life in history for the sake of affirming his ability to defy death by his own power, the Christian faith knows it to be impossible for man . . . to transcend the unity and tension between the natural and the eternal in human existence. Yet it affirms the eternal significance of this historical existence from the standpoint of faith in a God, who has the power to bring history to completion. . . .

[48] Heller, *op. cit.*, p. 219.

... Consummation is thus conceived not as absorption into the divine but as loving fellowship with God.[49]

Seymour Siegel, a leading contemporary Jewish theologian, speaks of Reinhold Niebuhr's interpretation of the resurrection of the dead as a profound theological insight that "can serve us as Jews in understanding our tradition." [50] Will Herberg offers an interpretation that parallels, from the Judaic side, the views of Reinhold Niebuhr. For Herberg, "Greco-Oriental" dualism is at once unfortunate and untenable. The teaching of resurrection avows that man's final destiny is not something he can claim as a possession, but rests solely upon the divine grace and mercy. It means "total dependence on God as against metaphysical self-reliance." Again, what is open to fulfillment is "not a disembodied soul that has sloughed off its body, but the *whole* man—body, soul and spirit—joined in an indissoluble unity." Finally, salvation is not a private affair that an individual can arrange at his death, "but the salvation of mankind, the corporate redemption of men in the full reality of their historical existence. The whole point of the doctrine of the resurrection is that the life we live now, the life of the body, the life of empirical existence in society, has some measure of permanent worth in the eyes of God and will not vanish in the transmutation of things at the 'last day.' The fulfilment will be a fulfilment for the *whole* man and for *all* men who have lived through the years and have entered into history and its making." We cannot dispense with the doctrine of the resurrection, "no matter how impatient we may be with the literalistic pseudo-biological fantasies that have gathered around it through the centuries." [51]

Again on the Christian side we have this passage from Rudolf

---

[49] Niebuhr, *The Nature and Destiny of Man*, Vol. II, pp. 295–297. Cf. Niebuhr, *Faith and History* (New York: Charles Scribner's Sons, 1949), p. 150.

[50] Seymour Siegel, "Reinhold Niebuhr: An Appreciation," *Conservative Judaism*, XXV, 4 (Summer, 1971), p. 60.

[51] Will Herberg, *Judaism and Modern Man* (New York: Farrar Straus and Young, 1951), pp. 229–230; see also pp. 50, 53, 70, 206, 236.

Bultmann: "Does the salvation proclaimed by the Christian message mean only the salvation of the individual, the release of the individual soul from the contamination of sin and from suffering and death? Or does it mean salvation for the fellowship of God's people into which the individual is incorporated? The fact that the earliest Church in its mission simply took the latter for granted essentially differentiates it from the propaganda of other oriental religions of redemption. . . . In Christianity, the individual believer stands within the Congregation, and the individual congregations are joined together in one Congregation—the Church." [52]

On the Judaic side, a related emphasis is forthcoming in the affirmation of the corporate people of God, Israel. The teaching of resurrection makes an equal place for man's individuality and his social and corporate character. And it undergirds the doctrine of the goodness of the entire creation, in contrast to a suspect "body" in the Hellenistic tradition. It is worth noting that the influence of Greek thinking has not prevented the Catholic Church from affirming, as was done at Vatican Council II, that while man is "made of body and soul," he is nevertheless one. And he "is not allowed to despise his bodily life; rather he is obliged to regard his body as good and honorable since God has created it and will raise it up on the last day." [53]

As I write, a most recent item of note is the prediction of Krister Stendahl, a New Testament scholar and Dean of the Harvard Divinity School, that the long tradition of speaking about the immortality of the soul is coming to an end. Against that teaching stands the doctrine of resurrection, with its concern for the triumph of the justice of God.[54]

[52] Bultmann, *op. cit.*, p. 93.

[53] "Pastoral Constitution on the Church in the Modern World," as cited in *The Catechism of Modern Man*, p. 70.

[54] Krister Stendahl, as cited in *The Christian Century*, LXXXIX, 5 (Feb. 2, 1972), pp. 115–116.

VIII

We see, then, how the eschatological nature of Judaism and Christianity could permit the entrance into the Judaic-Christian world of the extrinsic teaching of immortality (a development that might not have taken place had death as *finis* been the prevailing or only word) and yet how the two traditions have managed to keep the teaching of immortality from displacing the teaching of resurrection.

Our analysis has suggested certain reasons why the displacement could not occur. A most salient and persisting factor is the indissoluble union of *finis* and *telos* with morality. Eschatology means ethics; ethics means eschatology. "See, I have set before you this day life and good, death and evil" (Deut. 30:15). Righteousness is life; wickedness is death. In the face of death "there prevails the 'Thou shalt' as a triumph over the 'Thou must' of fate; there prevails the moral freedom that is always available to man, the 'acknowledgment of the judgment' which is his acknowledgment of the commanding God." [55] The tenaciously moral character of the Judaic and Christian traditions engenders abiding opposition to the notion of immortality, with that notion's openness to the irresponsibilities of amorality and its nourishing of pretensions to human purity. The doctrine of immortality is, in a word, an escape from reality.

But if the two traditions are preoccupied with the morality of men, they are no less faced by the question of the morality of God. For it is a shattering truth that human beings who give every evidence of righteousness and humility suffer and die along with the wicked. Because both faith-traditions assert the justice and goodness of God they cannot escape the issue of theodicy. Within the Judaic-Christian domain the raising of the question of theodicy will never cease, for the simple reason that no human being ever asks to be born or to be subjected to the specter of death. Suffering and death are existential questions for the non-

[55] Leo Baeck, *The Essence of Judaism*, rev. edn. (New York: Schocken Books, 1948), pp. 131, 137.

believer, just because he is a man. But to the believer, these questions must be addressed to God as well. Once upon a time, some Hasidim in Poland put God on trial. The basis of the charge was dismay over the way Jews were suffering. And the Hasidim convicted God.[56]

The theodicean impasse may be broken by virtue of an ultimate eschatological redress of evil and joyful mastery by good. The end (*telos*) is realizable in and through a final resurrection. Thus is the divine sovereignty vindicated. But what of the dignity of human creatures? Will the human cause be vindicated as well? It is said that a certain Hasid was asked whether he would forgive God for the loss of his wife and for other calamities. "Yes," he replied, "Today is Yom Kippur; I must forgive." [57]

The present reflections began on a note of paradox; they may end in the same manner. On the one hand, the tormented hope of some who today speak from within the Judaic and Christian traditions is not that they will never die but that God must not die; on the other hand, they yearn for God to die their small deaths at their side. Frederick Sontag asks of God, "Is his nature such that he may share in man's ultimate agony, death?" [58]

Who will win, in the end: Death or God? Faith and love join hope in the testimony that death is sentenced to death:

He will swallow up death forever, and the Lord God will wipe away tears from all faces, and the reproach of his people he will take away from all the earth; for the Lord has spoken (Isa. 25:8).

I heard a great voice from the throne saying, "Behold, the dwelling of God is with men. He will dwell with them, and they shall be his people, and God himself will be with them; he will wipe away every tear from their eyes, and death shall be no more, neither shall there be mourning nor crying nor pain any more, for the former things have passed away" (Rev. 21:3–4).

[56] Samuel Sandmel, "The New Movement," *Common Ground* (London), XXIII, 2 (Summer, 1969), p. 13.

[57] Elie Wiesel, *Souls on Fire: Portraits and Legends of Hasidic Masters* (New York: Random House, 1972), p. 108.

[58] Sontag, *op. cit.*, p. 136.

PSYCHIATRIC ASPECTS OF D
IN AMERICA

BY VIVIAN M. RAKOFF

No one has anything very original to say about death; the possible attitudes are as predictable and stereotyped as certain openings in chess games. They constitute a small repertoire: the stoical restated in the language of a particular time and society has as its only message, acceptance; the existential plucks from the certainty of finiteness an exhortation to savour life; and the death-denying philosophies of religion or political promise offer release through hope in either a spiritual or temporal future. There are subvarieties within these categories, and there is a perennial invitation to either obscurity or dialectical semantics in the face of the intractable problem. Death breaks the back of imagination and produces a spate of metaphor. True experiential phenomenology is almost impossible; [1] societies shuffle these philosophical possibilities to arrive at stereotyped public attitudes manifested in architecture and ceremonial as characteristic and as varied as pyramids, Italian monumental graveyards, Indian burning ghats, Parsee towers of the dead, aboriginal tree trunk burial,[2] wakes, or the smooth green lawns of Californian burial parks where only a small bronze plaque in the grass signifies the corpse beneath. But within these institutionalized stereotypes, individuals must still come to terms with their own deaths and imagine themselves into nullity. And in the act of private imagining, the philosophies and institutional attitudes find a final common path-

---

[1] Although there are sporadic anecdotal accounts of people who have died clinically and recovered or who have nearly died, about death itself they have little to say. R. C. A. Hunter, "On the Experience of Nearly Dying," *American Journal of Psychiatry*, Vol. 124 (1967–1968), pp. 84–88.

[2] R. Haberstein and W. Lamers, *Funeral Customs the World Over*, Milwaukee (Bulfin Printers, 1960).

way. It is hard to believe, in our private bewilderment, Tillich's [3] exhortation to move out of time into timelessness, Marcuse's [4] demand that death be refused as ontological essence, the mind-breaking word games of Heidegger [5] which end as an acrobatic denial of death, or Camus' [6] elegant confrontation with absurdity with its image of all doomed mankind supporting one another on their death raft: it is hard to believe that these help in any immediate fashion apart from giving form to the perennial preoccupation. Perhaps only religious belief in the absolute of continued personality and an after-life constructed on the template of the temporal world can give that comfort which allays primordial anguish.

America has its own death myths, its own way of coping with the terror. While the stereotype certainly lacks universal applicability, there is a dominant eschatology. There are still individuals and communities who mourn and memorialize as in Middle Europe or in the mainland China of the past, and who share the patterns of fear of death and belief in a possible afterlife [7] of traditional societies; but America conjured into its superficial stereotype is a country of the eternal now, of the young, face lifting, good teeth into the seventies, old ladies in Bermuda shorts, hair coloured at will, endless euphemisms for chronic disease, affliction and death.

America has few great public mausolea. Its memorials are memorials to the achievements of men, and by not being tombs, they sidestep man's mortality. There *is* Grant's small Grecian tomb overlooking the Hudson, and there are others scattered across the country, but the actual bones of the dead are not the centers of inspiration and pilgrimage. Even those egregious exceptions, the Kennedys, are buried in graves which cannot be

---

[3] In H. Feifel, ed., *The Meaning of Death*, New York (McGraw-Hill, 1959).

[4] *Ibid.*

[5] *Ibid.*

[6] A. Camus, *Le Mythe de Sisyphe*, Paris (Gallimard, 1962).

[7] D. Lester, "Experimental and Correlational Studies of the Fear of Death," *Psychological Bulletin*, Vol. 67, No. 1 (1967), pp. 27–36.

recognized as unique among the many on the Arlingto
And Feifel's [8] observation applies more to America than
else in the West: "In the presence of death Western cu
and large has tended to run, hide and seek refuge in group norms
and actuarial statistics. The individual face of death becomes
blurred by embarrassed curiosity and institutionalization."

Why is North America so particularly death-denying? There
are other highly developed industrial societies, other countries
which started off as colonial territories, other more or less atheistic
communities, other societies indeed which are less religious than
the United States. Why does it seem that particularly in America
the common Western denial of death and its concomitants,
finiteness, growing old, being sick, is so powerfully developed?

Prosperity and atheism are surely not sufficient answers. Where
does one look for reasons which are enough to give meaning to
such a "now"-oriented civilization? The clues are probably in
history, particularly those aspects of history which relate man to
the processes of time, tradition, and hope; to a great informing
myth which becomes part of the structure of belief and subse-
quently of action and world-view. The initial myth will in the
course of history be broken apart and reassembled, corrupted
and subject to entropic distortion, but if it is early enough and
sacred enough in the history of the group, it will color not only
public but private life. The *bricollage* of a great myth is only
possible for those who possess it unthinkingly.[9] The first great
myth of America is surely "coming to America," under special
circumstance and with special belief.

Other than Amerindians, every American family in modern
times begins with leaving the old people behind. The earliest
historical experience of the United States was a flight from the
customs and norms of the mother country. The past was well
left behind, and the wish in the United States was not to continue
the forms of the old society but to create a new one. The revolu-

8 H. Feifel, *op. cit.*
9 C. Lévi-Strauss, *The Savage Mind*, Chicago (University of Chicago Press, 1966).

tion came early in the history of the nation, and the revolution gave social expression to the geographic fact of distance and the long journey across the Atlantic culminating in a rejection of the past. The matrix of the anticipated future was laid ideologically in the self-conscious expression of the pursuit of happiness as an inalienable political right, and physically in the geographical platform: the apparent limitlessness of the continent, a stage for the expression of political and individual destiny. Toynbee,[10] writing on the turning away from Christianity in the seventeenth century, has emphasized that those who settled in North America were products of the primary tradition of dissent, as opposed to those who settled in South America as faithful children of their king and Church, for whom revolution came late and in fragmentary form.

In the history of families, social and political forces as they affect the parental figures become incorporated into the personal relationships and psychological adjustments of the children. A tradition of response can be traced through generations of a particular family.[11] And America has expressed the exigencies of its myth to each subsequent generation of immigrants. While it has failed to meld all groups and all norms into one, it has been a powerful assimilator of reminiscence which did not fit the dominant mores of an energetic, optimistic expansion. The myth had pragmatic success and was validated by reality: economic prosperity and geographic plenty and the hope of the expanding frontier all supported it. One may imagine that if the king lost his authority and the parent Church was seen only as tyrannical, and if the first families came, leaving the old behind weeping on the quay-sides, then those first mythical journeys may well have informed the subsequent history of a society which rejected the old, the ancestral and all past authority.

[10] A. Toynbee, *Man's Concern with Death,* London (Hodder and Stoughton, 1968), p. 122.

[11] J. Haley, "Speech Sequences of Normal and Abnormal Families with Two Children Present," *Family Process,* Vol. 6 (1967), p. 94.

The optimistic myth demands an awareness of the future and the denial of the historical. Existential psychiatric thinkers have characterized the time sense of the manic patient as being only in the present or the future. By contrast, the depressive patient is heavy with his past and incapable of seeing anything beyond his miserable present. This fits with everyday experience, where a good day and a good feeling are associated with a sense of things getting better and the possibility of the future. It is a truism that in North America the new model and the word "modern" carry overtones of desirability that are not only the result of economic cynicism and the exploitation of an ever-expanding market, but appear to be a genuine value system of psychological importance.

The old and the worn, whether people or things, are to be cast aside or left behind. It is assumed implicitly that the future holds expansion, plenty, and a constant process of psychological "becoming."

The lesson was well learned and native-born Americans responded to the frontier and its endless promise [12, 13] while the new immigrants clustered in the established centers. It seemed that the myth did have the power to mobilize action, and it served as a shield against the unknown dangers of a continent so vast that its physical space was in itself a metaphor of existence. In recent years the pattern of constant movement has become so universal that the average North American family is said to move once every five years. In this repetitive process the old continue to lose their integral place in the imaginative life of the family, they can no longer be nurturant figures, or figures with a hierarchical status one may aspire to. The family, by constant movement, has become anhistoric. When the old *are* admitted into the imaginative myth, they are at best sentimental-

[12] F. J. Turner, *The Frontier in American History*, New York (Holt, Rinehart and Winston, 1962).

[13] F. L. Paxson, *The History of the American Frontier*, Boston (Houghton Mifflin Co., 1924).

ized into soft, gentle, sexless creatures, who, precisely because their reality is denied, are given attributes which fit the wishful phantasies of their children—phantasies of an infantile order, without the quirkiness of flesh and blood experience. The granny of the advertisements provides cookies or goodies, or as in the recent series of Bell Telephone advertisements, can only be reached by long distance telephone. In another series of glossy advertisements, the aged live in retirement colonies where the sun shines perpetually (and in which death of the old among the old occurs with frightening casualness, and its traces are quickly covered up by rituals of denial that are the antithesis of the rituals of mourning).

A further consequence of the withdrawal from the old is that one cannot contemplate one's own aging with dignified equanimity, or benefit from the comfort of institutionalized forms for "being old." The comical pretenses of refusing to recognize age are perhaps the most corrupt fragments of the original hopeful myth: the frontier demands that one always be ready for the expanding future, and therefore not only actresses—whose economic necessities alter their requirements—but many others deny the ontological necessity of wrinkles and settle for an anonymous mask of tight skin, behind which roll the old eyes that cannot be newly-glazed. And the structure of downtown cities denies that the old and the feeble may wish to move among us; denies that we can be old in any decent public form while still in the world. The speed of traffic light changes prohibits easy walking for one who is slow; the height of the sidewalk above the street-level makes hopping up and down an effort. There is the absence of enough public toilets, the lack of benches in shopping centers, and housing developments and apartment houses that provide few facilities for the uninstitutionalized old.

Informing the banishment and sentimentalization of death is a horror of aging as unrealistic and as mythic as the idealization of the young.[14]   The stereotype of the old is social and sexual impotence, loneliness and dependence—an obscenity.   Certainly the evidence of ordinary experience is largely against this, and writing in this area is frequently couched as counter-polemic against the implicit assumption.   Recently one has been reassured that the old are not and need not be uncreative; that the old-age colony is not an aesthetic and social horror; that families do not entirely reject their older members; [15, 16] that the old retain considerable sexual vigour.[17]   But it is not the social reality which ties old age to death; it is the folk myth against which the polemic is directed.   For the folk myth is not to be too easily rejected. The plain fact remains, independent of optimism or pessimism, that old age does lead to death.

In his essay "The Ideology of Death," Marcuse rejects the stoical and existentialist acceptance of death as ontogenetic necessity, since to accept it is to accept bounds upon the degree of human hope: "The Metaphysics of finiteness thus falls in line with the taboo on unmitigated hope."   In his terms, acceptance of death is only one of the numerous manifestations of implicit psychological repression inherent in contemporary society, and liberation depends upon the rejection of all boundaries placed on human possibility, since we cannot know which of the limits of existence are the results of repression and which do constitute ontogenetic necessity.   But it happens ironically that in America —the principal target of Marcuse's criticisms—death has always been rejected as ontogenetic necessity.   This country has refused limitation, and contemporary medical technology, the product of the developed West as a whole, has given good support to this

14 T. Hickey and R. A. Kalish, "Young People's Perception of Adults," *Journal of Gerontology*, Vol. 23 (1968), pp. 215–219.

15 M. Clark and B. G. Anderson, *Culture and Aging: An Anthropological Study of Older Americans*, Springfield, Ill. (Charles C Thomas, 1967).

16 B. L. Neugarten, "Grow Old Along with Me! The Best is Yet to Be," *Psychology Today* (December, 1971), pp. 45–84.

17 W. H. Masters and V. E. Johnson, *Human Sexual Response*, Boston (Little, Brown & Co., 1966), pp. 223–260.

attitude and new achievements continue to give technological encouragement to the received myths of boundlessness and possible immortality. Frequent death in childbirth, the death of small children through inter-current illness, arbitrary and sudden death by infection or surgical emergency, which all at one time seemed part of the condition of man, are obviously no longer expected aspects of the ordinary. Cancer, heart disease and "the bomb" remain as reminders of mortality. But most cancer is a disease of growing older if not of the aged, and "the bomb" has become almost as mythic as death itself—ineluctable, under distant and arbitrary control, hovering in the wings of life. And if age or the appearance of age can be denied, or painted over, or pushed away, then these associated conditions have less power to rub one's nose in the reality of dying.

Over and above sickness and necessary decay, the human cell has a finite number of cell divisions programmed in its genetic code, and it is the genetic code which is finally the essence of ontogenesis. It is the irreducible substance of the given man and would seem to be the limit to which hope can be stretched. Still, the genetic code has been cracked, and it may indeed be possible to manipulate it, until the number of potential divisions of the human body's constituent cells is infinite. Or to pursue the technological phantasy further, the heart need no longer depend upon itself but *can* be programmed and boosted by skin-embedded prosthetic batteries and impulse providers. One could say that this is no different from the hearing devices which have been available for some time, or the artificial joints made of plastic and vitallum, or indeed the simple substitution for loss that is the wooden leg. But it *is* different: the heart as an organ of myth is not the equivalent of the ear, the hip joint or even the kidneys. Kidney transplants and skin transplants had been done before Christian Barnard transplanted the first heart in Capetown, but few laymen know the names of those surgical pioneers, or the name of Peter Medawar, Nobel Laureate, whose work on tissue acceptance and rejection has provided the scientific basis for this achievement, and transformed it from mere plumbing—skilful plumbing, it is true—but in action only plumbing performed on tiny, slippery flexible tubes. When one can have a reconditioned heart or even a borrowed new heart, then the true mythic boundaries of mortality have been pushed back even further. The perennial hope that we may indeed live forever—not as some abstract, ultimately spurious theological construct but actually in our bodies—seems a bit closer to realization. Clarke's vision of men as part flesh and part intricate machinery who have broken through into a new stage of evolution, and Buckminster Fuller's assertion that the voluntary actions of men are now a part of the process of evolution, raise the technological vision of control of human destiny to a level of grandeur decidedly above that of the expansion of a physical frontier.

But even before the reality of today's remarkable technology, Faustian medicine has held the subtle promise that eternal life might in a particular case be just possible. I recently heard what I believe to be an old joke: "No old Jewish person ever dies—he is always killed by the doctor." And so he is, if for "killed" one substitutes the words "not saved." "He was not saved by the doctor" is the negative side of the hope so elaborately bolstered in many hospitals, and which in its apparently humane intention has resulted in the inhuman practices of ministration to the dying patient about which Kubler-Ross [18] has written so movingly. The dying patient has become a challenge to the prevailing technical omnipotence, and it has been common practice to use uncritically any resuscitation and life-prolonging equipment a hospital happens to have available. Terminal transfusions, pumps, catheters, electrical pacemakers are, as Dr. Kubler-Ross

---

[18] Elisabeth Kubler-Ross, *On Death and Dying*, New York (The Macmillan Company, 1970, paperback edition). Her writing is essentially anecdotal, and one would wish to hear of more elaborate attempts to document the characteristic responses of Americans as compared with people in other societies; but this caveat aside, one must be grateful to Kubler-Ross for the attention she has brought to bear on our immediate practices in North America. Many hospitals and physicians have taken her lessons to heart and instituted a less omnipotent and more watchful approach to the dying.

describes them, applied to the body of the patient with an apparent disregard for his personality or his need to die calmly and with dignity. In detailing the process of dying from the time that the patient first becomes aware of the probably fatal diagnosis, Kubler-Ross emphasizes that the mores of American society fail to equip people to face either their own deaths or the deaths of those close to them. In her structuring of case histories, the patient passes through characteristic phases of denial and isolation, bargaining, and depression before reaching a relatively peaceful acceptance of inevitable death. It is essentially a pathway the individual must make himself, since the instruction of having watched someone close to one dying with calmness and stoicism, or having a socially elaborated set of rituals, is missing for most Americans. And the denial extends from the dying person himself to the mourners.

The elaborate funeral arrangements of America have been mocked and undertakers' business practices raked,[19] but the elaborate embalming, the curiously innocuous ceremonial, the euphemistic language continues in the absence of effective and accepted funeral ritual. At its extreme, the funeral ritual is constructed to deny all its most obvious implications. The painted face of the corpse staring back at the mourners from the satin headcushions of the elaborate coffin (coffin is a taboo word in these circumstances) reinforces a phantasy that "he has not died but only sleeps." The solidity and furniture-like quality of the coffin suggest a cozy and almost enviable retreat underground. Probably the most bizarre elaboration of this wish is the newly-discovered technological possibility of cryogenics [20] derived from the remarkable success of frozen food processing. The corpse is plunged into liquid nitrogen, until the day that "medical science has advanced sufficiently to restore the one in suspended animation back to life." Cryogenics has become not only a technique

---

[19] J. Mitford, *The American Way of Death*, New York (Simon & Schuster, 1963).
[20] M. McClintock, *Cryogenics*, New York (Reinhold Publishing Corp., 1964).

but a cult. And as a cult it is a logical elaboration of the technology of terminal care in a sophisticated hospital, an extension of the remarkable care which can maintain certain patients with brain damage, unconscious but certainly alive, for long periods of time.

Naive rationality is a poor guide to the rituals of mourning and denial a poorer one. Naive rationalists find themselves awkward and tongue-tied when faced with the simple human necessity of having to approach a person who has recently sustained the death of someone close to him. There is a mumbled greeting, a shake of the hand, and an awkwardness. Reason dictates that when someone has died, one should be able to say, "Well, he's dead. Now let's dispose of him and carry on with things." But that kind of reason is manifestly too simple, and ignores the complex network of relatedness which requires dissolution through the processes of mourning. Mourning is essentially a process of unlearning the expected presence of the deceased, a process more serious than the embarrassment referred to. The classical papers of Freud [21] and more recently of Bowlby [22] have emphasized the necessity of mourning rituals and the expression of grief for disentanglement from the deceased so that life can continue unencumbered by unresolved relationships. Without appropriate mourning, the dead cannot be allowed to die. The survivors, having denied death or not responded adequately to its reality, are caught in unresolved conflicts, are in fact "haunted." In this instance the recognition of death as a necessity for continuing life is not a trick of dialectic plucked from despair to give a measure of comfort; it is a necessary process of normative psychological functioning.

Unfortunately, neither individuals nor communities can readily

[21] S. Freud, "Mourning and Melancholia," in *The Complete Psychological Works* edited by J. Strachey, London (Hogarth Press, 1966), Vol. 14 (1917), pp. 237–242.

[22] J. Bowlby, "Childhood Mourning and Its Implication for Psychiatry," *American Journal of Psychiatry* (1961–1962), pp. 481–499.

create myth or ritual voluntarily. The best that can be achieved is a syncretic *bricollage* of previously elaborated mythology which may or may not be successful. In the absence of accepted processes of social mourning, the best that may be achieved is on the level of instruction: almost as a public health measure the facts regarding the necessity of mourning should be made widely known; the disservice that the funeral parlor's denial of death does to surviving families should continue to be publicized, and the rightness of expressing grief in passionate form encouraged. Perhaps by these devices the reality of death can be restored, and forms of mourning for the rational, the religiously *déraciné*, the culturally marginal, and so on, may grow organically into accepted institutionalized forms.

A less obvious and perhaps fanciful consequence of the mythic denial of the reality of death is possibly its reduction within the culture from lethal violence to the comical—comical in the sense that action in comedy has no true consequence and is the action of a game: Donald Duck fractured in one frame is restored in the next, and in the "Commedia," however tragic its content, the murdered king goes home to bed when the performance is over. If death is not perceived as a fundamental reality, then the consequence of interpersonal violence may be thought to be unreal. Lacking seriousness, murder and assault are perhaps given encouragement and license. It follows that it is not that the media encourage and create violence, but that the unconscious assumptions of omnipotence and ontogenetic optimism have encouraged the wish to believe that ultimately death is a fiction. But while the degree of American denial may be greater than that in other societies and while it has engendered profound social and personal energy, Americans are not unique in their wish to guard themselves against existential despair; they are not uniquely foolish or self-deluding. In the ancient Sanskrit epic the *Mahābhārata*, there is a text known to almost every Indian child: [23]

"Every day, every single day, men take up their places in the house of death,

Yet those remaining alive, still bring themselves to hope that they are made of unchanging flesh.

What could be funnier!"

[23] *Mahābhārata, Vanaparva,* chapter 314, verse 118 (Poona, Critical Edition).

BEING AND BECOMING DEAD

BY ERIC J. CASSELL, M.D.

Bᴀꜱɪᴄ to understanding the problem of caring for the dying is an awareness that with all its mysteries and ultimate questions, death is a concrete event, mostly smelly and mean, preceded and followed by pain.

The conflict of these two spheres of human thought—that concerned with being and meaning, and that concerned with the body—while finally resolved for the dying person, is brought into the open for those around him. In the physician who regularly attends the dying, the conflict finds constant, if subliminal, expression and is responsible for much of what troubles him in the care of the dying patient.

It appears that the modes of thought, the very mechanics of reason on which physicians have depended for generations and which have been so useful for understanding the body, may lead away from an understanding of dying. In other areas of medicine and science there is also a growing awareness of some of the inadequacies of analytic thinking (atomistic, particular, reductionist . . . that method of thought which reduces things into their parts in order to understand them). Nowhere is the failure so poignant as in death. Physicians are not alone in having accepted analytic thought as the only kind of reasoning "proper" for public usage and professional discussion. As science won its battle with theology far beyond A. D. White's [1] fondest hopes, a whole culture has accepted that the path to ultimate under-

---

[1] Andrew D. White, *A History of the Warfare of Science with Theology in Christendom*, 2 Vols. (New York: Dover Publications, 1960). (Original appeared in 1896.)

standing lies in analysis—dividing, breaking into parts, holding still. Meanwhile, synthetic thought, the other kind of thinking, (integrative, intuitive, magical . . . the mythical thought of Lévi-Strauss, the dialectic of Sartre . . .) innately appropriate to other parts of the human condition, has sunk into the privacy of each of us. Though atrophied by disuse, that necessary kind of reasoning continues to trouble the surface of comprehension.

In death and dying the two opposite kinds of thinking, the one (analytic) open and robust, the other (synthetic) private, and in this day, underdeveloped, bring conflict and paradox onto the scene.

Throughout this discussion we will see paradoxes and problems which I believe are best understood as dichotomous ways of thinking and states of being. Seen in this manner the care of the dying becomes more comprehensible. Hopefully, in examining this problem we will achieve clearer understanding of the two kinds of thought and their meaning to us.

Traditionally, in our culture approaches towards death have been religious or philosophical, but as in so many other areas, with the growth of technological society the voices of religion and philosophy have become remote. Not only do religion and philosophy seem distant from the bedside but their questions seem tangential in terms of modern physicians and what actually goes on. But how can it be that questions of morality and human values, so basic to the care of the dying, seem remote, "strange," or tangential in the actual setting of care?

To start answering that question, it is necessary now to address ourselves to death as a real event. It seems reasonable to start by defining what we mean by dying. Laymen, when asked "How would you define a dying patient?" generally divide death into physical and non-physical states. They say that someone can be dead in his mind. It is a concept quite familiar to us, and the connotation is unpleasant. Some quotes will illustrate: [2]

[2] The quotations come from taped interviews in the author's office.

Interviewer: "When do you consider somebody to be dying?"

Respondent 1:   "A person dies when the mind stops thinking."

Respondent 2:   "I had a sister-in-law who was a fantastic person . . . and led such a full life, and for everybody, and I just adored her. And she had a second marriage which was terrible—it demolished her, really. Just before, the day before she was going to go to a psychiatrist, she committed suicide. Yet I could see her dying, because her whole interest was gone. Is this what you mean? Is this what you're asking me . . . ?

Interviewer: "I'm asking you how you feel about it. In other words it is possible to be dying without having a disease?"

Respondent 2:   "That's right, yes, yes. This is what I'm saying."

Generally, the death state of mind is considered sad. Under special circumstances, however, it is seen as making physical dying easier; [3] take, for example, patients with terminal disease who know they are going to die and <u>withdraw interest from</u> the <u>world</u> around them. But for this discussion, the essential fact is that the non-physician sees the mind-body duality and usually considers a dead mind in a living body to be a bad thing.

Physically defining a dying person seems harder for the layman and, in searching for a definition, he looks into his own experience. Where experience provides example, the temporal relationship between *dying* and being *dead* is generally considered short; where experience fails to provide information there is some hesitancy, but again, the time between being dying and being dead is quite short. It is interesting that for many there is considerably greater confusion about physical death than about non-physical death. While many factors may enter into this confusion, from denial to simple ignorance, I believe it is an area where, as in illness, the confines of reason do not provide easy answers to the questions.

Two type cases, however, serve to illustrate the layman's defini-

[3] Elisabeth Kubler-Ross, *On Death and Dying* (New York: The Macmillan Company, 1970).

tion. Case one is that of a 42-year-old man who, feeling entirely well, was found after a routine blood test to have acute mye-loblastic leukemia, a disease whose prognosis is at best measured in months. Does the layman think the patient is dying? There is some doubt. Does the patient know? No, he doesn't and feels entirely well. Finally the respondents generally agree that he is not dying. If he knows, then he *may* be dying if he *thinks* he is, but confusion continues. Some quotes from respondents presented with this case illustrate the point:

Interviewer:	"Is he a dying man?"
Respondent 1:	"I guess on one level, yeh, I mean, he must be."
Interviewer:	"If you looked at him and knew he had leukemia, would you look at him and say there's a dying man?"
Respondent 1:	"Probably not."
Respondent 2:	"I think dying, real dying, implies a knowledge of death, of personal death."
Interviewer:	"So that person, that leukemic is not a dying patient?"
Respondent 2:	"No . . . I mean, if you mean his body is deteriorating, yes."
Interviewer:	"If you looked at him would you see a dying person?"
Respondent 2:	"No, no."

Case two is that of a man who has had four or five heart attacks. In his present one he is in an intensive care unit, unconscious. There are doctors and equipment surrounding him as in a scene from the most dramatic television show. Is such a patient dying? Again, some confusion—but it is generally agreed by laymen that such a patient is dying.

To summarize, the layman is quite clear about a mind-body duality in dying, and sharp and decisive in assigning the possibility of "mental" death. He is more confused and vague about the physical dying, as experience fails him, but generally assigns short periods of time to the process—attended by obvious and great functional loss.

The physician defines the dying patient very differently. First of all, he does not step quickly into the mind-body duality. He will concede, if pressed—or sometimes he will spontaneously offer the same concept as the layman—a dead mind in a living body, but it is not quick to his lips. The physician bases his definition upon the prognosis of the disease from which someone is dying. In so doing he is basing the definition upon his own ability to do something about it. By his own, he means literally his own, but also the collective ability of his profession. His definition of the dying patient is, therefore, dependent upon his knowledge and his technology.

To return to the two type cases again, the physician views them differently. Case one, the 42-year-old man with acute leukemia, is seen by the physician as dead the moment the diagnosis is made! It does not matter whether the patient knows or not—to the physician he is a dying man. On the other hand, the patient with the numerous myocardial infarcts around whom the many physicians and their machines are crowded *is not dying until he is dead!* The response of a surgeon clarifies the point: "A dying patient is someone that I can't help."

The difference between layman and physician in the definition of the dying patient is striking, and we begin to sense that the two may be speaking of two distinctly different states, two different kinds of being. To go further, it is necessary to examine more closely what the layman really means by the mind-body duality and the word dying. Several quotes are useful.

The first comes from a 38-year-old psychiatrist speaking of his own father. (He went on to make the usual physician's definition later in the interview.) He said: "My first thoughts are about withdrawal of interest, of cathexis—to use my fancy words—from the world. My father died way before he was dead, you know. He died when he stopped listening to the

Brooklyn Dodgers' baseball games—months before he was dead."

The second quote is from an interview with a 29-year-old woman. "A dying patient? Oh dear! I guess somebody who has given up the will to live and doesn't have any energy." A little later in the interview, she says, "There are those things that you really get sick with that can kill you—well, like we had this dog that was a perfectly healthy dog for nine years and my mother came home and he was dead—I guess he had a stroke, or something. But I guess he was never dying."

Thus the process of *being dying* may precede the process of *being dead*—or it may not ever occur. Being dying may not be present in someone about to be dead or may be present in someone not about to be dead. Doctors, then, have two distinct processes with which to deal: 1) the process of being dying, a nonphysical process, and 2) the process of becoming dead, a physical phenomenon.

The physical aspect—the process of becoming dead—has classically been the province of physicians and constitutes the manifest content of their work. The science that underlies our understanding of the body is a model of analytic thought. Over the centuries that have been occupied in the development of scientific medicine, doctors have, in essence, taken the human body apart bit by bit. It has been dissected into its parts with ever smaller discrete units being discovered as technology advanced. In the last century, to the previous anatomic dissection has been added the physiologic and chemical dissections of function. Each piece has been examined and understood in the belief, accepted by all, that by understanding the parts in their most minute detail, an understanding of the whole would be achieved.

In the course of this, physicians have learned to think in body terms. They see disease in the same terms, as altered units of structure or chemistry. But for our purposes it is important to conceive of the physician at the bedside thinking in *body* terms and to know that this is thinking in analytic terms. Whether the body is really best understood in these terms is not central to this discussion, but it is important.   There is a certain circularity to the process.   Analytic thought having been the thought mode in which the discoveries about the body were made, it is the kind of thought required to understand the results of the discoveries. In fact, there are problems in thinking about the body the way we do.   We tend to conceive of the organism as sets of static states, altered or otherwise, rather than to think about the transformation between states.   In practice this means that we have difficulty thinking in terms of function and think more easily about what may be less important—alterations in structure.   This has been phrased, in other fields, as a distinction between being and becoming, and analytic thinking brings one primarily to states of *being*.

Whatever difficulties may be presented by analytic thought, it has for physicians the advantage that it is depersonalized.   Part of the paradox of our subject is the constant opposite pull upon the doctor's mind.   Depersonalization is destructive, but without depersonalization there is not the objectivity essential to caring for the body.   *To understand physicians you must picture them straining in fascination to understand what is happening within the body beneath their hands.*   The process of becoming dead occurs in the depersonalized body.   But what do we mean by depersonalized?

In discussions by laymen, theologians and philosophers, one can commonly hear the belief and fear that doctors unnaturally extend or prolong the dying life toward their own ends or toward the ends of their science rather than act in a manner best serving the needs of their patients.   These discussions somehow imply that there is a distinction between doctors and other men; between the doctor and the man within the doctor—between "medical" values and "human" values.

It is an extremely interesting implication which seems to flow naturally from the distinction we have just noted between doctors and other men. But when doctors (or "medical" values) are said to be different from other men (or "human" values), it is more an accusation than a simple statement of fact (in contrast, for example, to the statement that poets are different from other men).

Let us, then, look more closely at the statement as an accusation. To do so we must return to the bedside. The setting which gives rise to the fear might be as follows. A 74-year-old man has been ill for a long time. In the beginning he had been stubbornly independent, and despite considerable pain and discomfort, carried on his life, making light of his illness. Recently the pain had become almost constant, his appetite failed, and his clothes hung on him. His once constant wit gave way to depressed silence. He moved into his daughter's house so that she could watch over him; even reading the newspaper seemed to require more effort and interest than he could spare. Finally, no longer eating, he was admitted to the teaching ward of a hospital. Soon he was part of the familiar scene of intravenous feedings, injections, and arduous diagnostic studies—all grinding on almost oblivious of him and his family. The pace of treatment hastened as he sank into coma. The family was at first grateful that the burden had been lifted from them, but they became increasingly angered at all the young doctors doing so much to the patient but giving them so few words. The family was angry, too, at the machinery clustered around his bed, and the bottles and tubing and wires connected to him. It was especially distressing because the patient himself had resisted going to the hospital, saying he didn't want to be "an experiment for them."

It would be common, in commenting upon this scene, to say that the family was upset because the doctors were so impersonal. To put it more strongly, we might say that the doctors had depersonalized their care of the old man: they were acting as if he were not a person, but an "it"—a living piece of flesh toward which every effort had to be extended to keep it alive. Seen in that manner (and, not infrequently, one hears people speak of physicians in those terms), the depersonalization has extended to include the patient himself. He too, although alive, has been depersonalized. In a mythical sense, a dehumanized object has been created that lives and breathes like a human being but is not perceived as a person.

Every act of the doctors is rational and follows implicitly from their present understanding of the disease process, the effects of treatment, and the workings of the body. The system of thought employed is clearly analytic reasoning. Remaining solely within that mode of thought, although there might be some—even quite wide—variation in individual acts, it would be difficult to conceive of any basic decisions that would have been essentially different. To have produced basic change in this hypothetical case would have required changing the very foundation of thought about the problem. Such change does not come easily.

In this case, at least in terms of the fear aroused in laymen, the analytic mode of thought (science) produced a monster. The case described here and the many similar ones that have given rise to present public distress are entirely creatures of current medical science, i.e., they were not possible even a few decades ago. It is of some interest to note, however, that although only present-day reality provides concrete example, the fear of a depersonalized living body is not new. The Frankenstein monster, Dr. Jekyl and Mr. Hyde, vampires, and a host of other fictional or mythical characters provide similar examples. The *golem* of Jewish mythology is a very old and well known example of a living body without a person within. Common parlance might say that these are creatures without souls.

From what has gone before and from this case we get a clue that the analytic thought mode may be essential to thinking about the body and, at the same time, antagonistic (reduced to its ultimate) to that mode of thought concerned with non-body, "human" values. Further, the possibility begins to emerge that the *body itself,* and "body values" in the setting of the dying patient, for example, may be antagonistic to non-body, "human" values. If so, we begin to see that the conflict between "medical" and "human" values and the conflict between the doctor and the man within the doctor is at a level so basic that it involves the very mechanics of reason and conflicting states of being.

The process of *being dying,* in contrast to the process of *becoming dead,* is an intensely personal, non-physical process. In what part of us does the process of being dying take place? The primacy of the body in serious illness is clear, but as we listen to our patients when they are well and when they are dying, it would seem that trapped within the ever-narrowing confines of the body becoming dead may be a person whose life continues on (our respondents clearly tell us this) and to whom the body is largely irrelevant—as is the case in health. Health, at least in part, incorporates the ability of the self to soar; allied with but unhampered by and unaware of the confines of the body. In a sense, illness, and certainly death, represent a defeat for the self within the body. Bodies can be conceived of as dying, but persons cannot. ✓

On the other hand, as in the cases of the respondent's sister-in-law whom she could see dying "because her whole interest was gone" or the psychiatrist's father who "died way before he was dead" as he withdrew interest from the world around him, the self can also be seen as dying independently of the body. ✓

No richer picture of the destructive effects on living that result from an injured relationship between self and body comes to mind than that so beautifully written by Lifton [4] in his study of the survivors of Hiroshima. There, in those unable to transcend it, the self remains shackled to a body seen as somehow already dead or permanently tainted in some inexplicable way. The interrelationships of the two independent but inseparable parts of being— the symbiotic halves of existence—humble us by their mystery and complexity.

But the two are so intricately bound together in the sick and the dying that if we are to care for them, we cannot rest in awe before the mystery. The concept itself is so urgent that it insists upon being understood. For that understanding, analytic

4 Robert J. Lifton, *Death in Life* (New York: Random House, 1967).

thought seems inappropriate. Although several generations of research on the mind and on social interaction, done increasingly in the analytic mode, have provided ever greater comprehension of aspects of thinking, the intimate nature of being remains elusive. In fact, the more analytic investigation becomes, the further "being" retreats. For the personal nature of being, synthetic thought seems more appropriate. However, synthetic thought is infinitely more difficult to comprehend. Perhaps that is the first characteristic of synthetic thought that strikes us—its seemingly inexplicable nature. It is that same characteristic that seems to make it, in this age of science, unacceptable for public discourse. It is the thought of Socrates' *daimon;* the flash of problem-solving in Kohler's ape, Sultan; the substance of insight, creativity and intuition; the basis of "sudden illumination." We see it from the outside; we know that it exists within us and in others, but we do not know what has taken place or how. It is clearly integrative thought—drawing upon and integrating into one response material from different levels of mindfulness, such as experience, the results of analysis, beliefs, feelings, insight, intuition, unconscious resolution, and so on. But the formula for the integration, the different values given to the parts of mindfulness that make up the synthetic thought remain a mystery to us, even as we have the thought. Unlike analytic thinking, in which we can, together, trace the path of our common thought, here the detailed path of thought is closed and only the result may be apparent.

Lévi-Strauss, in *The Savage Mind* [5] shows us, in considerable detail, how the two modes of thinking interact. As the notion is dispelled that the primitive mind is occupied *only* by synthetic thought, we can see some reason why our own synthetic thinking has become, in part, relegated by us to the primitive, the child, and the savage within us.

---

[5] Claude Lévi-Strauss, *The Savage Mind* (Chicago: The University of Chicago Press, 1966 [date of translation]).

By now it must be clear that analytic thinking and synthetic thinking cannot be valued one above or below the other but are better seen as two necessary and inseparable companions in the mind, just as self and body are companions in existence.

Because synthetic thought draws its results from so many levels, both personal and universal, it is the thought mode of human values and moral action. One cannot arrive at human values by analytic thought. In the same manner it is the mode of thought of shared human experience—of empathy. The mystery of it draws us on, as it has so many others over the ages until we begin to believe that the self *is* the totality of thinking.

However, for our purposes in understanding the dying, the following should be clear: Synthetic thought is real, and because it is integrative in nature, it is the opposite of analytic thought. It is the thought of human values and of shared human experience. Finally, in part because of its present low status, but mostly because of its private nature, its operation is not consciously manifest—we do not know we are thinking it. Further, the two processes—the physical process of *becoming dead* and the non-physical process of *being dying*—are represented, broadly speaking, by two different kinds of thought.

We can see that the doctor, in caring for the dying, is using two competing systems within himself to render care (as distinct from caring). However, although the two processes are distinct, they are so intimately entwined that if the doctor confines himself to dealing only with the process of becoming dead, he creates the depersonalized technological spectre with which the philosophers and the rest of us are concerned. But further, he gives up his function as a healer in favor of his function as a curer.

In a previous essay (*Commentary*, June 1970), I have discussed the function of healing as being concerned primarily with taking care of the non-disease elements that make up sickness, and the present tendency of physicians to flee the greater personal burden of being *healers* for the lesser intellectual burden of merely *curing.* [Curing is a technological pursuit, healing is a non-technological pursuit engaging primitive and as yet largely unexplored areas within patient and doctor.]

The healer provides a connection between the shrinking world of the sick and the larger reality of the well. He offers his own personal intactness to protect the sick person from the danger of having lost his sense of personal invulnerability. The healer's system of reason encompasses illness and offers the security of knowing to the patient for whom sickness is the fearful unknown. The healer provides a surrogate control of the world to the ill person whose own sense of mastery over his destiny may be slipping. And all of this is usually buried below words and unavailable to conscious processes.

But in all the ill there is a larger battle, the battle with death. No matter that it is probably not an unknown like death that we fight but rather, helplessness, whose fearful impotence we have all experienced in infancy. What matters is how large the fear. That battle is the healer's province. In our culture the picture of the physician doing battle with death is so well known as to need no elaboration, and the image goes back to well before the present era of therapeutic achievement. For the physician-healer the process is emotionally demanding and draining; the more challenging, the more draining the battle. For this reason he must save his energies and try only to engage where success is possible. Where success is not possible, healing gives way to the duty simply to "comfort and company" the dying.

Separating the physician-healer from the physician-curer is, of course, essentially artificial since there is no such absolute separation among doctors themselves. But it is not hard to recognize the validity of the concept and apply it to reality, where, indeed increasingly, doctors lean toward the less demanding, primarily intellectual function of physician-curer. The physician as curer does battle with blood counts and electrolytes. Freed from the very real constraints of healing, there is no limit to his field of battle.

Thus the human and ethical problems are, in part, created by the separation of the functions of healing and curing. However, as we have seen earlier, these two functions of physicians can be seen to occur within opposite and competing modes of thought: the analytic mode used by the curer and restricted by its nature to the physical process, the synthetic mode of thought more important in the function of the healer. We saw before how in the dying patient himself the two systems compete.

But the body *does* have ultimate sovereignty, and that is the basic dominion of doctors. The physician cannot enter the field of dying without being part of what can be seen as the battle between the body and the self within the body. We want the doctor, we require him, to take the part of our body—if he does not, he fails us. But if he *only* takes the side of the body, he also fails us.

Thus, to the previous dimensions of the function of the healer we must add the resolution of conflict between self and body in the sick and the dying. *It is essential to any understanding of doctors to realize that they, and they alone in society, are responsible to both the body and the self within.* And within the physician himself, if he is really engaged in caring for the dying patient, the same battle between body and self must be raging. This is the price of caring for the dying—the more so in this day when the analytic mode of thought is so well developed within doctors whereas the language of self lies largely unacknowledged and underdeveloped.

To summarize, we have seen how modern science can create a living body shell whose self is gone. But further, although literally a creature of today, the fear of the empty body goes far back in history. With that knowledge in addition to what we hear patients express about death and sickness, we see increasingly the validity of conceptually separating these two parts of being.

We have also seen how the two parts of the duality seem to be represented by two different kinds of thinking, and in physicians by two different functions, healing and curing. For understanding we must see the two parts for what they are, but for man to be whole, the two must blend.

> "But O alas, so long, so far,
> Our bodies why do we forbear
> They are ours, though they are not we,
>   We are
> The intelligences, they the spheres
> We owe them thanks, because they thus,
> Did us, to us, at first convey,
> Yielded their forces, sense, to us
> Nor are dross to us, but allay.
> On man heavens influence works not so,
> But that it first imprints the air,
> So soul into the soul may flow
> Though it to body first repair.
> As our blood labors to beget
> Spirits, as like souls as it can,
> Because such fingers need to knit
> That subtle knot, which makes us man."

From *The Ecstasy*
John Donne

HOW OTHERS DIE—REFLECTIONS
ON THE ANTHROPOLOGY
OF DEATH

BY JOHANNES FABIAN

Mes larmes ne la ressusciteront pas.
C'est pourquoi je pleure.

Anonymous French Epitaph *

Death seems to be a harsh victory of the species over the definite
individual and to contradict their unity. But the particular individual is only a *particular species being,* and as such mortal.

Karl Marx **

I

IN recent years, anthropologists were consulted—and often gave
profuse advice—on such vital American problems as war with
exotic societies, or aid to exotic societies; rural and urban poverty;
the intricacies of ethnic identity; ecology and the use of drugs;
marriage, divorce and promiscuity; or simply the future of the
species. In many instances, societal interests, expressed in patterns of funding for research, were quickly translated into conceptualizations and theories and have in some cases given rise to
subdisciplines and professional alliances of the secret society type.
Department chairmen, having to sell their discipline to tightfisted
university administrators, proudly point to rising enrollment
figures. Often, and probably correctly, this is interpreted as a
shift from introductory philosophy, literature and history to

---

* From Robert Sabatier, *Dictionnaire de la Mort* (Paris: Albin Michel, 1967).
"My tears will not bring her back to life. This is why I am crying." All transla-
tions are my own, unless indicated otherwise.

** Karl Marx, *Economic and Philosophic Manuscripts,* D. J. Struik, ed. (New York:
International Publishers, 1964), p. 138.

anthropology as a provider of a *Weltbild* to undergraduate freshmen.

Why is it, then, that in recent years anthropologists have had little to say about death? With few—and rather doubtful—exceptions, we cannot report on any major ground-breaking work.[1] Therefore it seems that, at this point, the anthropologist's contribution toward understanding death in modern society can only be made in a roundabout way, as a self-searching examination of an aspect in the discipline's history, a history which, of course, is situated in the social and cultural context of the society or societies which produce anthropology.

A negative question (Why do anthropologists *not* speak about death?) has its logical pitfalls. Imagination simply offers too many reasons when one tries to account for the absence of things. But the question may set an historical trap which might be even more dangerous. Students of death in contemporary society appear to agree on the fact that modern man "suppresses" thinking about death.[2] It is tempting to see in anthropology an accomplice of presumed societal interests in suppressing death. The possibility cannot be ruled out since it has been demonstrated for other issues and areas such as colonialism, racial discrimination and the control of the poor (although there remain founded claims to the contrary). But to transpose attempts at understanding to the level of ethical-moral accusations (and confessions) is the worst kind of obfuscation that can be perpetrated on any intellectual enterprise, since it can only create self-righteousness, not self-understanding.

[1] A cursory check of four major professional journals revealed that between 1960 and 1970 only nine "death-related" papers were published, and the majority of these dealt only with the purely ceremonial aspects of death. Concerning major monographs, the situation is not much better. The few that appeared within the last decade or so (Warner, Goody, Gorer, Douglass) have been widely recognized but cannot claim a trend-setting influence. Let me note, however, that Goody's study contains a wealth of information and suggestions which make it valuable beyond its declared limits.

[2] To point to but one prominent example, see R. L. Fulton and Gilbert Geis, "Death and Social Values," in *Death and Identity*, edited by R. L. Fulton (New York, 1965), pp. 67–75.

Hope for clarification and critical examination would seem to lie in our ability to relate our negative rhetorical question to positive barriers to communication, to practical impediments and normative prohibitions. It will be the contention of this paper that, while some of these may be understood as direct reflexes of a present social context, others—and more important ones—will have to be sought in the intellectual history of the discipline and in the history of the use to which anthropological findings have been put in other contexts, notably in philosophical, psychological and sociological approaches to death in modern society.

II

Our attempt to understand that development will be guided by the following thesis: Much like the concept of culture, approaches to death in anthropology have undergone a process of parochialization. Parochialization has had the effect of eliminating a transcendental and universal conception of the problem. "Death" (in the singular) has ceased to be a problem of anthropological inquiry; there are only deaths and forms of death-related behavior.

In his essay on "Matthew Arnold, E. B. Tylor, and the Uses of Invention," George W. Stocking revealed—and debunked—one of anthropology's favorite myths: that Tylor with his definition of culture (in 1871) became the father of modern anthropology in the sense that he provided the discipline with its relativist and strictly scientific foundations. He is supposed to have brought the study of culture out of a haze of humanist appreciation of human achievements into the light of non-evaluative, systematic investigations of man's cultural products. But Stocking maintains:

> Far from defining its modern anthropological meaning, he simply took the contemporary humanist idea of culture and fitted it into the framework of progressive social evolutionism.[3]

[3] George W. Stocking, *Race, Culture and Evolution* (New York, 1968), p. 87.

The humanist idea of culture and the notion of social evolutionism are the reference points between which we have to place the origins of a transformation of anthropological inquiry into death. J. G. Frazer clearly combined them when he wrote in one of the introductory chapters to his *The Belief in Immortality:* [4]

> The problem of death has very naturally exercised the minds of men in all ages. Unlike so many problems which interest only a few solitary thinkers, this concerns us all alike . . .

But from a humanist "us" he imperceptibly switches to an evolutionist "they":

> Some of their solutions of the problem, though dressed out in all the beauty of exquisite language and poetic imagery, singularly resemble the rude guesses of savages.

For Tylor and Frazer alike, evolutionism remained a frame of self-identification, a means of locating one's own society at the peak of human intellectual development. In a seemingly paradoxical way this resulted in steering anthropological inquiry away from universal problems of human existence to concern with particular products of evolution. For Frazer the "problem of death" became a matter of studying particular savage customs, leading him to embark on one of his *tours de force* around the ethnographic globe. [5]

A further step in the parochialization of anthropological inquiry can be recognized in the position Franz Boas developed in violent opposition to evolutionism (and therefore inevitably

---

[4] James George Frazer, *The Belief in Immortality and the Worship of the Dead*, Vol. I (London, 1913), pp. 3, 31f.

[5] It is interesting to note that 19th century evolutionism could become a conceptual vehicle for a theologian in his search for a "positive" meaning of death. In the light of the theories of Darwin and Weismann, death is discovered as the "servant of life" (Newman Smyth, *The Place of Death in Evolution*, New York, 1897, p. 14), a "secondary event" in the course of life whose necessity is nothing but a form of adaptation following the law of natural selection (*ibid.*, p. 27). Echoing our epigram from Marx, Smyth states "that the duration of life for the individual members of different species seems to have been determined upon the principle of utility, for the preservation of the species" (*ibid.*, p. 33).

accepting many of its tenets). Boas shared with Tylor and Frazer a view of the importance of "customs" in the study of culture and human thought (cf. Stocking, *op. cit.*, p. 221), but he was concerned with their "tyranny" rather than their curiosity value. As Stocking notes, this in fact led to an identification of culture with folklore, a profound change in concept.[6] Once the anthropological concept of culture had lost its universal (albeit elitist) character, it was clear that the discipline simply no longer had a theoretical plane on which to face challenges such as the problem of death. Anthropologists had ceased to answer for humanity; their investigations had left the field of tension which is created when particular phenomena are related to universal concepts or processes (be it the 18th century's Natural Law, the *Geist* of the romantics, the natural laws of evolution, or even the Universal History of the diffusionists). Having lost a universal frame of inquiry, questions having to do with the nature and meaning of death had to be implanted (if not buried, if the pun be permitted) in various parochial "units" of research which came to replace that frame. In fact, Hertz's classical study, "Contribution à une étude sur la représentation collective de la mort" (see note 21), conceived in the line of Durkheim's powerful attempt to base a universal theory of knowledge on a parochial conception of the social nature of man, has remained the last generally significant contribution to guide social anthropological research (and even that one has been largely outside the horizon of Anglo-American anthropology until its recent reception in a translation).

To be sure, classical authors of modern anthropology continued to assert convictions of their predecessors. Echoing Tylor and Frazer, B. Malinowski admits that these "orthodox views" of the experience of death as the core of primitive religiosity "are on the

---

[6] ". . . Boas' equation of folklore and culture had implications for the idea of the "culture" of civilized men. Just as folklore at the primitive level tended to be seen as encompassing culture, so also the culture of more advanced peoples was now largely seen as folklore" (Stocking, *op. cit.*, pp. 225f.).

whole correct." There is at least a core of an earlier universalism preserved when he states:

> Even among the most primitive peoples, the attitude towards death is infinitely more complex and, I may add, more akin to our own, than is usually assumed.

But all this must be seen in the perspective of his own theoretical progress beyond "orthodox views." Malinowski was among those who advanced a parochialization of anthropological inquiry by first isolating religion from intellectual life in general:

> Thus the belief in immortality is the result of a deep emotional revelation, standardized by religion, rather than a primitive philosophic doctrine.

That was a radical departure from Tylor's views. Secondly, there is Malinowski's idea of religious ceremonies addressed to the experience of death as "self-contained acts, the aim of which is achieved in their very performance," which, lastly, led him to define the scope of anthropological inquiry in a way that has remained exemplary:

> The ceremonial of death which ties the survivors to the body and rivets them to the place of death, the beliefs in the existence of the spirit, in its beneficent influences or malevolent intention, in the duties of a series of commemorative or sacrificial ceremonies— in all this religion counteracts the centrifugal forces of fear, dismay, demoralization, and provides the most powerful means of reintegration of the group's shaken solidarity and of the re-establishment of its morale.[7]

Later criticism and quite important modifications [8] notwithstanding, this encapsulation of the experience of death in self-

---

[7] Bronislaw Malinowski, *Magic, Science and Religion* (Garden City, N. Y. 1954), pp. 47, 51, 52. In support of my contention that this view became paradigmatic, see David G. Mandelbaum, "Social Uses of Funeral Rites," in *The Meaning of Death*, H. Feifel, ed. (New York, 1959), pp. 189–217.

[8] Notably by Meyer Fortes, *Oedipus and Job in West African Religion* (Cambridge, 1959).

contained acts, performed for the sake of a self-containing social unit, had the intellectually disastrous effect of opening to anthropology an easy escape from the "supreme dilemma of life and final death" (Malinowski). The argument is this: Beyond all differences in theoretical and methodological inclination, social-cultural anthropologists may be presumed to be students of human behavior inasmuch as it is determined by cultural orientations (among other things). Death as an event is the termination of individual behavior. Therefore there cannot be an anthropological study of death, but only of behavior toward death as it affects those who survive. It must be a study of "how others die" in more than one sense: examining the reactions of survivors and interpreting these reactions through ceremonies, ritual practices, ideological rationalizations—in short, as "folklore." Whether this is intended or not, death-related behavior will then be placed at a safe distance from the core of one's own society.[9]

I hasten to emphasize that this is not the whole story, although it describes the most influential orientations [10] in the discipline. We should give recognition to dissenting views [11] and examine the possibilities of an anthropology of death which faces, rather than escapes from, the "supreme dilemma." But first we must consider yet another context in which anthropological inquiry into death appears to have been forced into the position of a spectator of, rather than participant in, social reality. We should at least note that in this context we are unable to do justice to a more profound theoretical issue concerning an epistemological

[9] A classical and extreme formulation of that position may be found in A. L. Kroeber, "Disposal of the Dead," *American Anthropologist*, 29 (1927), pp. 308–315, in which he classes mortuary practices with such peripheral phenomena as "fashion."

[10] Attesting to that power is, for instance, Clyde Kluckhohn's essay "Conceptions of Death among the Southwestern Indians," in *Culture and Behavior*, R. Kluckhohn, ed. (New York, 1962), pp. 134–149, which begins with a sensitive formulation of the problem, looks to Boas for guidance, and ends with a Malinowskian statement. A more recent example may be found in the conclusion of William A. Douglass' study of funerary ritual in a Basque village, *Death in Murelaga* (Seattle, 1969).

[11] The classical reference for such dissent has become Clifford Geertz, "Ritual and Social Change: A Javanese Example," *American Anthropologist*, 59 (1957), pp. 32–54.

conception of "the other." It is raised by Donald T. Campbell in his discussion of the foundations of behaviorist versus introspective psychology. Similarly, our cursory sketch of the parochialization and folklorization of anthropological inquiry should not give the impression that the notion of "primitive" otherness has always and necessarily had a stultifying effect. On the contrary, in the tradition of the Enlightenment *philosophes,* anthropologists such as Lévi-Strauss (see section V of this paper) and Diamond have employed it in a critical fashion. As Diamond argued, "the authentic historian [which is what he thinks an anthropologist must be] . . . . approaches other societies in other times with the confidence that his humanity is equal to the task of registering *differences.* And that, though not the only element, is the *critical* one in all human communication." [12]

III

In one form of the Roman games (the *munera*), alien and exotic people were put to death by other exotic people or animals. Similarly, fascination with the curious, the violent, and the exotic seems to be the arena assigned to the use of anthropological studies of death by analysts of contemporary personality and society. Among the many examples that could be adduced to support that observation, I should like to point to Talcott Parsons. In his essay, "Theoretical Development of the Sociology of Religion" (first published in 1944), as well as in *The Social System,* it is the problem of death which causes him to turn to Malinowski's "classic analysis" of Trobriand funeral rites, and to W. L. Warner, E. E. Evans-Pritchard and C. Kluckhohn and their studies of death in relation to witchcraft. The point is that here

[12] Donald T. Campbell, "A Phenomenology of the Other One: Corrigible, Hypothetical, and Critical," in *Human Action: Conceptual and Empirical Issues,* Theodore Mischel, ed. (New York, 1969), pp. 41–69; Stanley Diamond (ed.), *Primitive Views of the World* (New York, 1964), p. xv.

the issue of death is not one among many occasions to turn to anthropology but, with few exceptions, the only one.[13]

While our metaphorical allusion to the Roman games [14] captures much of the rationale for appealing to anthropological studies of death-folklore, we should not overlook a number of theoretical reasons which led investigators of death in modern society to assume the role of spectators of the "primitive." Most importantly, the turn from the "us" to the "they" was taken by anthropologists themselves, as we tried to show in the preceding section. In part it was dictated by their basic evolutionary perspective, by that imperceptible transformation of culture into folklore, and by all sorts of murky mixtures of racism and colonialism which, often unconsciously, imposed themselves on seemingly objective analyses. But these tendencies appear to have been reinforced and codified when philosophers, psychologists and sociologists put ethnographic reports to use in their own approaches to death. "Primitive" reactions to death may then be consulted for the purpose of illuminating ontogenetic development with parallels from man's early history.[15] Or, more fre-

[13] Talcott Parsons, *Essays in Sociological Theory*, rev. edn. (Glencoe, Ill., 1963), pp. 204f., and *The Social System* (Glencoe, 1951), pp. 304, 311. Other references in the latter to Malinowski (pp. 328, 469) and to R. Firth (p. 33) are again in the context of magic, i.e., exotic behavior, while only G. P. Murdock on kinship (pp. 154, 170) and A. Kroeber on culture growth (pp. 336, 488) appear to be recognized on predominantly theoretical grounds.

[14] A recent interpretation of the Roman *munera* suggests, however, that the link may be more than just a metaphorical one. With the connivance of Roman intellectuals these games were presented to a people "who had lost the habit of forging its own history and was now content to participate, in their Sunday's best, in a parody . . . . the weapons of the gladiators and the techniques of combat borrowed successively from defeated peoples served as the fossilized image of the Roman conquest." (Roland Auguet, *Cruauté et Civilisation: Les Jeux Romains* (Paris, 1970), pp. 238f.)

[15] To name a few examples from otherwise highly perceptive philosophical treatments, Plessner writes: "The empty forms of time, space, self, and death have in common the fact that they presuppose a detaching act of objectivization; they can be attained only by the type of human being who has become conscious of his individuation. By contrast, children and primitive peoples meet death, and indeed the phenomenon of disappearance as such, unselfconsciously and without wonder." (Helmuth Plessner, "On the Relation of Time to Death," in *Man and Time* (Papers from

quently, we will find attempts to identify contemporary reactions to death, especially those that appear irrational, overly ritual and picturesque, as survivals of "archaic" forms. However, essentially the same connection may be made for an inverse argument: that what is wrong with modern man's relation to death is the absence or suppression of these ancient ways of coping with its threat. Usually without critical examination, these "primitive" reactions to death are placed in the domain of religion (which in turn is taken to constitute a self-contained aspect of human activity) and this makes it possible to replace the general evolutionist perspective with a view of "secularization," religious devolution, as an intrinsic component of modernity. Primitive and folkloric death-customs may then be located in a nostalgic past— which is yet another way of relegating reactions to death to "the others," or at least the other that has survived in us.

Recently, Werner Fuchs published a study entitled *Images of Death in Modern Society* [16] in which he offers a tantalizing combination of astute criticism and simple acceptance of the very syndrome we are trying to describe. His point of departure is an observation which, I am sure, must be rather disconcerting to modern social-scientific students of death. Upon closer examination, it turns out that sociologists and psychologists who make "suppression" of death the cardinal topic of their analyses (here he refers to Fulton and Gorer) are in fact arguing very much like Christian theologians who lament modern man's apparent indifference to death. The suppression hypothesis, Fuchs argues, is an interpretation supported more by interests in preserving the vanishing influence of religious institutions than by empirical facts (pp. 7–14). In his own approach he dissociates himself

---

the Eranos Yearbooks, Bollingen Series xxx-3), edited by Joseph Campbell (New York, 1957), pp. 233–263). The idea is implicit in the way Morin juxtaposes Piaget's work on children and Leenhardt's findings in Melanesia (Edgar Morin, *L'homme et la Mort*, rev. edn. (Paris, 1970), p. 31), or when Choron puts "primitives" into the company of animals (Jacques Choron, *Death and Modern Man* (New York, 1972), Appendix 2).

16 Werner Fuchs, *Todesbilder in der modernen Gesellschaft* (Frankfurt, 1969).

from such conservative culture-criticism for which death has become the "last trump" (p. 8) against secular, industrial society. On the one hand he rejects the idea of death as a constant; on biological as well as social grounds it can be shown that man's increasing power over nature has made such a notion obsolete. On the other hand he takes it upon himself to demonstrate that modern man does not simply suppress his reactions to death. He may submit to death as a fact, but he has preserved many of the ancient ways, symbolic and ritual, of coping with that experience. This is the point where he is compelled to turn to anthropological studies of primitive death-lore in order to create a background and contrast for his views of the genesis of modern images (pp. 26–50). There is no need for us to criticize extensively his use of anthropological concepts and findings, for he himself anticipates objections when he admits to the analogous and abstract nature of his arguments (e.g., pp. 26f., 50f.). It suffices to point out some of those assertions which we take to confirm our thesis that anthropological studies of death have been, by and large, assigned the role of providing the exotic "other" to the sociologist's "we."

First we find, as expected, the "folklorization" of primitive culture in a formulation worth quoting at length:

> It stands to reason that in primitive societies such ideas [of death] will not be found as opinions and attitudes but always closely linked to the institutional field in which death is symbolized. Images of death in primitive societies can hardly be identified as relatively independent intellectualizations [als Geistiges] but only in and with social institutions in which the group attempts to socialize death (p. 38).

Secondly, Fuchs is compelled—by his assumption that emerging modern images are determined by notions of a "natural" and "peaceful" death—to project into primitive reactions the violence we would expect to be associated with the exotic spectacle of dying: primitive man related to nature not by mastering it, but through "magical" interpretation (pp. 46f.); the helplessness and oppressive nature of primitive socialization in turn resulted in violence (p. 47). The mere frequency of violent death must have led to a kind of confusion between dying and killing (pp. 48f.). Death is experienced as interaction and hence can be induced by social agents (e.g., in the forms of Voodoo death and similar phenomena, p. 49). It would be easy to show that speculations of that kind are not at all borne out by what present anthropology and prehistoric archeology tell us about the ecological adaptations of "primitive" man or the role of violence and the history of warfare. In any case, Fuchs' argument must be read backwards. Primitive reactions to death are bound to be seen as magic-exotic and violent because they serve as points of departure in a series of developments toward "rational" (natural and peaceful) images of death.

Appeals to anthropological findings in this study and in many comparable ones have little more than projective value. They express more about the spectators than about those who are being watched.

IV

It appears that progress in understanding will depend on our ability to free the notion of death from its encapsulation in behavior, custom and folklore and to restore the experience of the termination of individual life to its full problematic status. This would call for an anthropology for which social reality and subjective participation in that reality are irreducible conceptual poles of inquiry. One would have to reject the use of anthropological research for the sole purpose of illustrating "socializations" of death, especially all those utilizations of ethnography in which the *analytical* notion of socialization is transformed into *programmatic* socialization, i.e., into support for contemporary recipes for coping with death.[17] To pose social and individual

---

17 This transformation was observed and made a point of critique in a comment of Alvin Gouldner's: "Over and against man's animal mortality, Parsons designs

reality as irreducible conceptual poles implies that the thrust of anthropological inquiry must be directed toward "mediations" between them. Above all, it entails an epistemological orientation which approaches conceptualizations and institutionalizations of death experience as *processes*, as productive "constructions of reality" rather than disembodied schemes of logic or social control.

Without trying to suggest systematic connections where there are none, we shall explore a number of intellectual contexts in which we see the potential for such processual approaches. First, however, we shall take up the case of modern prehistoric archeology since it may help us to determine more exactly what we are looking for.

More than twenty years ago, Edgar Morin began his *anthropologie de la mort* by observing that research in the process of hominization has been guided by two important kinds of evidence: the use of tools, and the burial of the dead (Morin, *op. cit.*, pp. 19f.). In the decades that followed, our image of early man has undergone considerable change. The timespan allotted to the process of hominization has been enormously expanded and at the same time former generic distinctions, often based on the scantiest evidence, have become blurred. Today, "Neanderthal" man, at first codified as the *Urmensch* in evolutionary scientific classification and popular iconography, turns out to be a much closer relative of modern man than we ever expected.

a 'social system' that, with its battery of defenses and equilibrating devices, need never run down. What Parsons has done is to assign to the self-maintaining social system an immortality transcending and compensatory for man's perishability. It is thus that Parsons' social system extrudes all embodied mortal beings and, indeed almost any kind of perishable 'matter,' and the system is instead constructed of 'role players' or roles and statuses that transcend and outlive men. Much of Parsons' theoretical effort, then, is, I suspect, an effort to combat death. But it does entail a denial not only of the death of individuals, but also of the death of society and, particularly, American society." Alvin W. Gouldner, *The Coming Crisis of Western Sociology* (New York, 1970), pp. 433f. One does not have to share Gouldner's position (especially not his contention that Parsons is the chief villain in the story) to see some of the deeper practical reasons for assigning to anthropological findings on death the theoretical value we found to be exemplified in Parsons' *The Social System*.

Nevertheless, evidence for burials has lost little of its theoretical importance. It may no longer be invoked as "proof" for achieved hominization since such a notion has become meaningless, but it has retained its crucial role as a phenomenon involved in hominization as a process. Thus in a recent analysis of Mousterian and Upper Paleolithic materials, Sally R. Binford sees in burials evidence for "new forms of social organization," "leading to the appearance of fully modern man." [18]

Of course, prehistoric archeology has been and will be under severe limitations due to the precarious nature of preserved evidence, no matter how much progress is made in the quantitative analysis of even the tiniest bits of data. Edgar Morin rightly cautioned against the "platitudes" which might be derived from a suggestive association of tool use and burial rites, i.e., of technology and symbolic activity. There is little use, he argues, in declaring that the tool humanizes nature and that notions of an afterlife humanize death, as long as the "human" remains a concept suspended in thin air. Rather, one should start with the assumption that "death, as does the tool, affirms the individual; it prolongs it in time as the tool extends it in space; (and the assumption) that it, too, strains to adapt man to the world and, by virtue of that, expresses the same lack of adaptation of man to the world, and the same conquering potential of man in relationship to the world" (op. cit., p. 20). It is easy to see that modern prehistoric research with its fixation on linear "adaptation" would react uneasily to so paradoxical a proposition. Yet it is because Morin accepts the epistemological frame we sketched earlier that his evaluation of prehistoric evidence does not take the folkloric turn. Notions of death and afterlife are not merely seen as customary expressions of man's functional conquest of death. Death, he maintains, "is assimilated to life" and filled with "metaphors of life" and ritual action based on and elaborating

18 Sally R. Binford, "A Structural Comparison of Disposal of the Dead in the Mousterian and the Upper Paleolithic," *Southwestern Journal of Anthropology*, 24 (1968), pp. 139–154. This paper should be consulted for a review of earlier, mostly French, literature on the importance of burial evidence in prehistoric research.

these metaphors, is action which "modifies the normal order of life" and reveals in the prehistoric and ethnological material a "realistic consciousness of death" (*op. cit.*, p. 22).

There is no sign that these propositions were taken up in the theoretical development of prehistoric research on burial customs. On the contrary, one can observe an increasing functionalization of burial evidence, making it more and more derivative of socio-economic relationships (while preserving its methodological importance).[19] All this amounts to a theoretical "socialization" of death in man's early history. The theoretical counterpart of such functionalization, by the way, seems to be an almost phobic avoidance of "catastrophism," i.e., of the violent, sudden termination of certain societies or cultural traditions as an explanation for discontinuities in the archeological record. While contemporary society seriously contemplates (and inflicts) societal death in war, in the nuclear threat and in the doom of ecological catastrophe, the New Archeologists appear to picture man's early history as continuous adaptation and growth within which individual as well as societal death is entirely subordinate to processes of social differentiation and ultimately to the law of selection. "Death as the servant of life" is a notion which places neoevolutionary theory in a curious vicinity to evolutionary theology, old (as in Smyth's *Death and Evolution*) and new (as in Teilhard de Chardin's all-embracing visions). If these observations are correct, then they suggest an interesting counterpoint to a tendency noted earlier. Whereas analysts of contemporary man and society project exotic, and often violent images of death into the human past, students of that human past offer naturalistic, adaptive and systematic explanations which are in contrast to the erratic and

19 This trend, as well as the theoretical and methodological sophistication which can be brought to it, is exemplified in a recent collection of papers edited by James A. Brown (*Approaches to the Social Dimensions of Mortuary Practices, Memoirs of the Society for American Archeology No. 25;* published as *American Antiquity,* 36, No. 3 (1971), part 2), especially in the contribution by Lewis R. Binford. The latter contains an interesting critique of Kroeber's paper (1927) which we cited as typical of the folklorization of burial customs (note 9).

violent preoccupations of contemporary society. With this, the general contention of this paper—that the historical development of anthropological inquiry into death has had a self-cancelling effect—acquires yet another dimension.

Our interpretation would of course be unfair and outright wrong if we should leave the impression that nothing was gained in the course of that history. "Folklorization" and functionalization of primitive culture have produced an impressive number of detailed reports on human reactions to death. Evidence for variation as well as for the persistence of certain general themes should make it once and forever impossible to revert to anemic, abstract notions of a gradual evolution "away from death." Nevertheless there remains the task of placing the problem of death back into the context of a "we," of its universal significance as well as its particular expressions, of its unmitigated threat as well as its achieved domestications. To achieve that transposition it will not suffice to revive the *Totentanz* motif of death as the great equalizer. Rather, we shall have to explore and develop the avenues which the discipline provides for breaching the gaps created by self-inflicted parochialization and imposed exoticism.

V

From the vantage point from which this essay is being written—contemporary anthropology in its more "humanist" and historical-critical orientations—there appear several theoretical confluents with a potential for leading an anthropology of death beyond its present confines. None of them is without predecessors in the history of the social sciences; their innovative power at the present time rests with the challenge they can bring against those entrenched tendencies we have tried to characterize.

The first example I find is Lévi-Strauss' radical structuralism. He, more than anyone else among the leading figures in current anthropology, has prepared the way back from a folklorized

ethnography of death into investigations of its universal significance. To cite but one statement of his:

> When an exotic custom fascinates us in spite of (or on account of)
> its apparent singularity, it is generally because it presents us with
> a distorted reflection of a familiar image, which we confusedly
> recognize as such without yet managing to identify it.[20]

Written in a tradition which had produced one of the classical
studies of the problem,[21] Lévi-Strauss' *The Savage Mind* addresses
itself to the issue of death in three contexts: the elementary contrast of life and death as expressed in the symbolic use of color-
contrasts (pp. 64f.), the role of names in marking an individual's
position in a community consisting of living *and* dead (pp. 191ff.),
and the significance of material reminders of the dead in providing "contact with pure historicity" (p. 242; see also pp. 236ff.).
Far from being relegated to the function of opening comforting,
self-contained ritual escapes, death-related customs are in this system analyzed as crucial evidence for the constitution of the "savage
mind" (which, it will be remembered, is studied not as a defective
but as a pure form of the human mind). In each case death is
seen as the *mediator* between the living and the dead and is
given a seminal role in the construction of those systems of
classification which govern man's natural, social and historical
universes. The existentialist critic may resent the intellectualist
and seemingly abstract character of that notion of death. But it
is one which restores the universal significance of primitive conceptions of death (many of which Lévi-Strauss sees realized in his
own society, cf. pp. 200f., 238f.). His investigations are addressed
to all of humanity, and especially the chapter on names, bearing
the intriguing title "The individual as a species" (Ch. 7, pp. 191–
216) could be read as a commentary to Marx's enigmatic statement with which we prefaced this paper.

[20] Claude Lévi-Strauss, *The Savage Mind* (Chicago, 1966), pp. 238f.
[21] Robert Hertz, "Contribution à une étude sur la représentation collective de la
mort," *L'année Sociologique*, 10 (1905–06), pp. 48–137.

Objections have been raised against Lévi-Straussian structural-ism in general and, implicitly or explicitly, against the analyses we alluded to. Some concern his empirical basis, others the epistemological foundations of his thought and yet others his ways with "structuralism." We share many of them and we are inclined to express them with more conviction the closer they relate to our own areas of competence. Yet it takes a task like the present one to recognize the power and potential which the structuralist trend in anthropology (at least in its original inten-tions) might have for undoing the parochialization of inquiry and the folklorization of culture we perceived as major obstacles to a non-trivial anthropology of death. For what it is worth, we may add a quotation from Lévi-Strauss which contains the startling proposition that anthropology is *nothing but* the study of death:

The world began without the human race and it will end without it . . . Man has never—save only when he reproduces himself—done other than cheerfully dismantle million upon million of structures and reduce their elements to a state in which they can no longer be reintegrated . . . "Entropology," not anthropology, should be the word for the discipline that devotes itself to the study of this process of disintegration in its most highly evolved forms.[22]

We can credit Lévi-Strauss with vindicating the logical nature of human reactions to death or, conversely, with vindicating death as the supreme mediator of those oppositions and contradictions by means of which the human mind constructs its universes.[23]

Put in slightly different terms, we may say that structuralism pro-vides for a possibility of viewing human experience of death as the core of a language, of a universal code. This is a far cry from previous fixations on exotic customs. Yet there remains a legitimate and fruitful concern in the anthropological tradition—the search

22 Claude Lévi-Strauss, *Tristes Tropiques* (New York, 1967), p. 397.

23 Some of the intellectual origins of that position should be sought in Hegel's philosophy of death; see Morin, *op. cit.*, pp. 262 ff.

for the *specific* message, the "what" that may be expressed in the language of death.

This brings us to the question of the "meaning" of culturally defined reactions to death. We should note at once that this problem, too, is by no means a new one and that consequently one would have to work through much accumulated rubble in order to get at its more productive and promising formulations. For one thing, search for meaning has at times been inseparable from a search for "functions" seen either as directed action or as measurable effects of action. Culturally specific forms of reacting towards death were then interpreted as implementations of beliefs in souls, in immortality, or in supernatural powers. Or they were perceived as ritual redress of crises inflicted on the group, as an oblique way of exercising control over the living (in the complex of "ancestor worship"), or simply as means of providing mental hygiene, individual and social, in the face of events which cannot be coped with through direct rational and instrumental action.

This is perhaps the best place to point to the important work of an anthropologist continuing a tradition to which we paid little attention in this paper: the conceptualization of death as a rite of passage. Victor W. Turner, in his study of Ndembu ritual,[24] shares our contention that a gap between a "we" and an exotic "they" is a prime obstacle to understanding (pp. 3, 6), and that rituals ought to be approached as language, or as a "semantic," as he puts it (p. 10). The wider conclusions he draws from his analysis should be sufficient to dispel an impression which our admittedly somewhat anti-ritualist critique of the anthropology of death may have left with the non-initiated reader.

Paraphrasing a statement which Geertz makes about religion, we may stipulate that a cultural reaction to death

is sociologically interesting not because, as vulgar positivism would have it . . ., it describes the social order (which, insofar as it does,

[24] Victor W. Turner, *The Ritual Process* (Chicago, 1969).

it does not only very obliquely but very incompletely), but because . . . it shapes it.[25]

The essay from which this quotation is taken remained in many respects in the frame it attempted to break (and probably had to in order to have this effect), but it has been crucial in preparing the discipline for a formidable task: to discern in the exotic and the folkloric that which reveals, in Morin's formulation, a "realistic consciousness of death."

There are various directions in which further inquiry may proceed. Common to all of them are the following basic orientations:

(a) A processual, constitutive view of culture and, consequently, of cultural conceptions of, and reactions to, death. "Primitive," no less but also no more than modern ways of coping with death can be realistic only to the extent that they can be shown to constitute praxis, active transformation and elaborations of concepts which are open, so to speak, at both ends: toward the crude experience of the termination of life and toward the impact of those sublime formulations which give meaning to that event. Recently Roy Wagner proposed a view of processual, innovative metaphorization as an approach to culture and found the following formulation immediately relevant to our problem:

> The ultimate dogma, known to all cultures, is that of mortality, the inevitability of personal death, and it follows that the most powerful innovative constructs will be those which achieve their force against this kind of human limitation. Hence it is that ghosts, gods, and other religious creations are so often represented as being omnipotent, omniscient, and immortal. Insofar as these beings are constituted as innovations upon a universal state of man, they are of necessity represented anthropomorphically, as metaphorical people who share man's active, causational capacity but not his mortality or his other limitations. Most effectively they take the form of innovations upon living human beings, and achieve their metaphoric status through acts of impersonation,

[25] Clifford Geertz, "Religion as a Cultural System," in *Anthropological Approaches to the Study of Religion*, edited by Michael Banton (London, 1966), pp. 1–46. The material cited appears on pp. 35f.

the metaphorization of social role, whereby a person is "extended" into the role of a ghost or deity. Man's life-course can be seen as the ultimate social role, which subsumes all others, and it is at this level of generality, that of man as a whole being, that religious impersonation as a form of innovation takes place.[26]

(b) A dialectical model of socio-cultural reality. This is implied in the criterion of "openness." Realistic conceptions of death could not be formed if the social world were seen as a self-contained domain. For a social conception of death to emerge, the event of individual death must be recognized as an inalienable mediator, not only in the Lévi-Straussian logical sense, but also in the phenomenological sense according to which subjectivity remains an irreducible pole in the construction of a social world. We may illustrate this position with a quote from Alfred Schütz in which he states

> that the whole system of relevances which governs us within the natural attitude is founded upon the basic experience of each of us: I know that I shall die and I fear to die . . . It is the primordial anticipation from which all the others originate. From the fundamental anxiety spring the many interrelated systems of hopes and fears, of wants and satisfactions, of chances and risks which incite man within the natural attitude to attempt the mastery of the world, to overcome obstacles, to draft projects, and to realize them.[27]

Schütz' phenomenology of the social world has been applied by Ilona H. Fabian to an analysis entitled *The Concept of Time in Zulu Myth and Ritual* (unpublished M.A. thesis, University of Chicago, 1969). There it is argued that conceptualizations of, and relationships with, the dead are crucial in the formation of a person's as well as a society's historical consciousness. The "I," the "we" and the ancestors are all seen to be involved in a constant process of mythical formulation and ritual action, resulting in an interpretation of "ancestor worship" bearing little resemblance to entrenched magico-religious or sociologistic explanations.

---

[26] Roy Wagner, *Habu* (MS scheduled for publication in 1972, Chicago), p. xx.
[27] Alfred Schütz, *Collected Papers I,* edited by M. Natanson (The Hague, 1967), p. 228.

(c) A communicative approach to ethnographic reality. This, again, should be understood both in the structuralist sense which holds that all of culture is a system of communication (and that death, being a seminal "distinctive contrast," is a prime datum of communication), and in the sense that any study of "others" is possible only on the basis of an inter-subjective context. As far as anthropological research is concerned, that context can usually not be presumed to exist but must be constituted in the process of producing ethnographic knowledge. As I have argued else-where,[28] this leads methodologically to a preoccupation with "lan-guage-centered" approaches. But more importantly, by including the ethnographic "other" in a communicative "we," it makes possible and necessary a critical, self-reflective anthropology. After all, attempts to breach the gap between the "we" and the "they" would probably end in egocentric delusions if they could be achieved by a simple act of good will, or a theoretical dictate. Redirecting the program for an anthropology of death from the stance we found to be dominant in its tradition to the problem of "how we die" does not rid us of the labors of careful ethnographic observation, comparison and analysis. However, it burdens these labors with the knowledge that, in working out an anthropology of death, we strive toward a realistic consciousness of death—ours.

VI

If our assessment of past and present developments is at least moderately accurate, we should be able to derive some rules for the interpretation of anthropological literature on death.

1. Ethnographic data cannot simply be adduced for the purpose of "explaining" antecedent forms of present attitudes, or to ac-count for exotic survivals in present attitudes, or generally to

[28] Johannes Fabian, "Language, History and Anthropology," *Philosophy of the Social Sciences*, 1, pp. 19–47.

support an evolutionary view of the history of death-related behavior. The reason is that a great deal of that ethnography has been selected, shaped, and interpreted precisely in terms of these research interests. There is at least the danger that one explanation (that of contemporary attitudes toward death) may be supported by something that poses as evidence (ethnography of "primitive" attitudes) but is in fact another explanation. *Mutatis mutandis,* the same rule applies when ethnographic support is sought for explanations of ontogenetic developments, such as the role of ideas of death in the process of individuation, especially when this is done to retranslate ontogenetic notions into schemes of history. Critical anthropology can offer nothing to support the thesis that the history of attitudes toward death has been one of increasing individualization and personalization. All this does not mean that ethnographic data cannot ever be subject to historical interpretations (be they historical in the traditional sense or be they processual-systematic in terms of a theory of evolution), but to determine their applicability calls for a degree of competence the average user of anthropological lore does not have. For any serious analyst of modern society, anthropology should be anything but a source of facile illustrations.

2. To touch on a more specific point, it cannot *a priori* be assumed that the "primitive's" reaction to death, because of his deep roots in a relatively small and well defined society, are any more specific and "meaningful" than those of modern man. Sensitive, critical ethnography may come to the surprising conclusion that "everything that touches upon death is equivocal, ambiguous" [29]—as we should expect it would be if there is some validity to the conception of death as a mediator of knowledge and meaning. How else could anticipations of death in thought and experience become the sources of innovative thought?

[29] J. Theuws, "Le styx ambigu," *Problèmes Sociaux Congolais,* 81 (1968), p. 33. For Theuws' attempt to place conceptions of, and reactions to, death into a wider context, see also "Naître et mourir dans le rituel Luba," *Zaïre,* 14 (1960), pp. 115–173.

3. Furthermore, one should not turn to anthropology if he is looking for proof that primitive man's life was much more under the influence of his beliefs in an afterlife and in the dead. To assess that influence one would have to specify its nature. Anthropologist-*cum*-psychologist Roger Bastide, for instance, points out that African traditional religion *externalizes* its dead and therefore can live with them, whereas Western society *internalizes* the dead in the form of obsessions and compulsive behavior. He comes to the surprising conclusion that

> if the structure of African cultures is that of a dialog [between the living and the dead]—then the structure of Western society is that of a monolog, but the monolog of the dead.[30]

4. Similarly, ethnographic evidence cannot easily be appealed to in support of culture-critical allegations that modern man, and modern man only, "suppresses" death because his secularized society does not give him mythical and ritual outlets for his reactions. Again, notions of primitive ritualism and of the all-pervasive sacredness of primitive man's world must at least be suspected of having been codified in reaction to the same economic and religious changes to which analysts of contemporary society link modern images of death (after all modern anthropology originated in that society).

5. Generally, one may predict that the "use" of ethnography to support schemes of evolution or devolution should become

---

[30] Roger Bastide, "Religions africaines et structures des civilisativns," *Présence Africaine,* 66 (1968), p. 104. This and other quotations used in the concluding section are selected for the suggestiveness of formulations, not as proofs for our position. Furthermore, I should like to express my acute awareness of the fact that this paper does not really take up the challenge of alternate views of death expressed, for instance, in the great traditions of China, India, and the Near East. Even anthropologists have, by and large, not dared to relegate them to a "primitive" status. This essay, then, is critical *within* one tradition of thought but perhaps not sufficiently critical *of* it. Given the magnitude of even the limited task of an immanent criticism, I can only hope for indulgence.

more and more difficult the closer the outside analyst gets to contemporary anthropology (hence the heavy reliance on early ethnography exemplified in the study by Fuchs quoted above).

This brings us to one last observation. As we see it, there simply is no way of getting directly at "the others." Anthropologists and other analysts of modern reactions to death must find or construct a meta-level of interpretation if they are to share their findings. In the late nineteenth century, this may have been the idea of a natural science of man in search of universal laws of progress to be verified by ethnographic "data" whose "objective" otherness was not seriously doubted. Today we seem to be left with the task of constructing a social hermeneutic, an interpretation of social reality (no matter whether it is "primitive" or "modern") which conceives of itself as part of the processes it attempts to understand. Lévi-Strauss was right: the anthropology of death is a form of dying, or of conquering death—which, in the end, may be the same.[31]

[31] My gratitude is due to Barbara Jones, Juli Skansie and George Bangs who, as my students, gave me the opportunity to clarify my ideas in the course of a seminar on death. An earlier version of the paper was read by several colleagues who offered encouragement, many necessary suggestions for improvement, and strong critical reactions. I wish to thank Francis K. Hsu, Clifford Geertz, Roy Wagner, Bob Scholte, Michael Meeker and, most of all, Ethel Albert.

NOTES ON CONTRIBUTORS

TALCOTT PARSONS is Professor of Sociology at Harvard University. Among his published works are *The Structure of Social Action, The Social System* and *The System of Modern Societies*. He is currently at work on *The American Societal Community*.

RENÉE C. FOX is professor of Sociology at the University of Pennsylvania. Her numerous publications include "Training for 'Detached Concern' in Medical Students" with Harold Lief. She is currently researching a sociological analysis of the Congo to be entitled *The Intelligence Behind the Mask*.

VICTOR M. LIDZ is a sociologist at the University of Chicago. He has previously published (with Talcott Parsons) "Death in American Society," and is preparing studies on the theory of moral-evaluative culture.

DAVID GUTMANN, Professor of Psychology at the University of Michigan, is the author of many articles, among which are "Mayan Aging—A Comparative TAT Study" and "Changes in Mastery Style with Age: A Study of Navaho Dreams," both published in *Psychiatry*. He is engaged in cross-cultural studies in traditional societies on the comparative psychology of aging.

HAROLD BLOOM, Professor of English at Yale University has published a number of works on poets and poetry, including *Shelley's Mythmaking, Blake's Apocalypse, Yeats,* and *The Anxiety of Influence*. In 1973 his latest work, *Wallace Stevens: The Poems of Our Climate* will appear, and he is at work on *The Native Strain: American Romanticism*.

WILLIAM F. MAY is Professor and Chairman of the Department of Religious Studies at Indiana University. He has published articles in the journal *Christianity and Crisis*, a volume entitled *Perspectives on Death*, and is now preparing essays on both religion and politics, as well as another book on the subject of death.

A. ROY ECKARDT is Professor and Chairman of the Department of Religion at Lehigh University. His previous publications include *Christianity and the Children of Israel* and *The Surge of Piety in America*, as well as numerous articles in scholarly and professional journals. He is now working on a book entitled *Speak the Truth in Love: Essays for Christians and Jews*.

VIVIAN M. RAKOFF is Professor and Director of Post-graduate Education, Department of Psychiatry, University of Toronto. He has previously published articles on family psychiatry, the neurophysiological aspects of addiction, and stoicism in politics, and is presently preparing a monograph to be entitled *The Cult of Spontaneity in Psychiatry and Politics*.

ERIC J. CASSEL, M.D., a practicing physician, is Clinical Professor of Public Health at Cornell University Medical College. He has published numerous articles and is currently preparing a work entitled *Studies in Medical Humanism: Belief and Value Structure in Patients and Physicians*.

JOHANNES FABIAN is Assistant Professor of Anthropology at Northwestern University. His previous works include *Jamaa: A Charismatic Movement in* ... *and Anthropology and Interpretation* (in press) ... is currently ... study of labor consciousness among African ...

SELECTED SCHOCKEN PAPERBACKS

History & Political Science

ANDRESKI, STANISLAV	Parasitism & Subversion
BERNSTEIN, EDUARD	Evolutionary Socialism
BROGAN, D. W.	Abraham Lincoln
CROSLAND, C. A. R.	The Future of Socialism
EINSTEIN, ALBERT	On Peace
GANDHI, M. K.	Non-Violent Resistance
GOSSETT, THOMAS F.	Race—History of an Idea in America
GREGG, RICHARD B.	The Power of Nonviolence
HILL, CHRISTOPHER	Puritanism and Revolution
MADARIAGA, SALVADOR DE	Bolívar
MÉTRAUX, ALFRED	History of the Incas
NORDHOFF, CHARLES	Communistic Societies of the United States
OLSON, MANCUR	The Logic of Collective Action
RAPOPORT, ANATOL	Strategy and Conscience
TOCQUEVILLE, ALEXIS DE	Democracy in America, 2 vols.

Sociology & Anthropology

BIDNEY, DAVID	Theoretical Anthropology
BREITMAN, GEORGE	The Last Year of Malcolm X
BROTZ, HOWARD	The Black Jews of Harlem
COOLEY, CHARLES HORTON	Social Organization
DU BOIS, W. E. B.	Dusk of Dawn
DU BOIS, W. E. B.	Suppression of the African Slave-Trade
FRAZIER, E. FRANKLIN	The Negro Church in America
HIMES, NORMAN E.	Medical History of Contraception
LA BARRE, WESTON	The Peyote Cult
READ, HERBERT	To Hell With Culture
SARTRE, JEAN-PAUL	Anti-Semite and Jew
SPIRO, MELFORD	Kibbutz—Venture in Utopia
ZBOROWSKI & HERZOG	Life Is With People: Culture of the Shtetl

Religion & Philosophy

ADAMS, JAMES LUTHER	Paul Tillich's Philosophy
ENSLIN, MORTON	The Prophet from Nazareth
KIERKEGAARD, SØREN	Stages on Life's Way
MARX & ENGELS	On Religion
RENOU, LOUIS	Religions of Ancient India
SUZUKI, D. T.	Outlines of Mahayana Buddhism
WEIGEL, GUSTAVE	Churches in North America
WOLFSON, HARRY AUSTRYN	The Philosophy of Spinoza, 2 vols.

Jewish Life and Religion

AGNON, S. Y.	Days of Awe
BAECK, LEO	The Essence of Judaism
BAMBERGER, BERNARD J.	The Story of Judaism
BUBER, MARTIN	The Legend of the Baal-Shem
BUBER, MARTIN	Tales of the Hasidim, 2 vols.
CHAGALL, BELLA AND MARC	Burning Lights
GLATZER, NAHUM N.	Franz Rosenzweig
GORDIS, ROBERT	Koheleth—The Man and His World
HERFORD, R. TRAVERS	The Ethics of the Talmud (Pirke Aboth)
IDELSOHN, A. Z.	Jewish Music
LEVI & KAPLAN	Guide for the Jewish Homemaker
KAPLAN, MORDECAI M.	Judaism as a Civilization
ROTH, CECIL	History of the Jews
RUBIN, RUTH	A Treasury of Jewish Folksong
SAMUEL, MAURICE	The World of Sholom Aleichem
SCHAUSS, HAYYIM	Guide to Jewish Holy Days
SCHOLEM, GERSHOM G.	Major Trends in Jewish Mysticism

American Experience

Arien Mack

In this book of essays that surveys American attitudes toward death
from the perspective of different disciplines, Talcott Parsons, Renée
C. Fox, and Victor M. Lidz explore the notion of life as a gift and its
implications for medical practice. David Gutmann, a psychologist, then
examines the American attitude toward aging, and Harold Bloom analyzes
the reverberations of death in American poetry. Two articles discuss
death's religious and philosophical dimensions: one by William F. May
and another by A. Roy Eckardt. The psychiatric aspect of death is dealt
with by Vivian M. Rakoff; and Eric J. Cassell, a practicing physician,
considers dying and treating the dying. Finally, Johannes Fabian, an
anthropologist, offers some contrasts in "How Others Die." This is a
major collection on an issue of immense current concern.

SCHOCKEN BOOKS
200 Madison Avenue
New York City 10016

Designed by Joe Caroff

ISBN 0-8052-0409-1